THE REVOLUTIONARY PROGRAM THAT HAS WORKED FOR MILLIONS CAN WORK FOR YOU!

Now you can attack any managerial problem with *double* the skill, intelligence and effectiveness. *THE SILVA MIND CONTROL METHOD FOR BUSINESS MANAGERS* shows you how to relax and tap your inner source of creativity—to use *all* your potential for business success!

ABOUT THE AUTHOR

One of the true pioneers of mental training, José Silva spent 22 years developing his widely acclaimed Silva Mind Control Method. Today he is chairman or president of five corporations, including the worldwide Silva Mind Control International, Inc., which he founded. Since 1966, his program has helped more than four million people in 55 countries utilize their whole mind to live and work with greater intelligence, ease, and success.

Books by José Silva

The Silva Mind Control Method
   (with Philip Miele)
The Silva Mind Control Method for
  Business Managers
   (with Robert B. Stone, Ph.D.)

Published by POCKET BOOKS

THE SILVA MIND CONTROL METHOD FOR BUSINESS MANAGERS

JOSÉ SILVA

IN ASSOCIATION WITH
ROBERT B. STONE, PH.D.

PUBLISHED BY POCKET BOOKS NEW YORK

POCKET BOOKS, a division of Simon & Schuster, Inc.
1230 Avenue of the Americas, New York, N.Y. 10020

Copyright © 1983 by Prentice-Hall, Inc.

Published by arrangement with Prentice-Hall, Inc.
Library of Congress Catalog Card Number: 83-13888

ISBN: 0-671-61110-0

First Pocket Books printing June 1986

10 9 8 7 6 5 4 3 2

POCKET and colophon are registered trademarks
of Simon & Schuster, Inc.

Printed in the U.S.A.

Dedicated to the people who read this book,
who perform the mental exercises to activate more
of their mind, and who, as a result, help make this
world a better place in which to live.

About the Authors

José Silva never attended a day of school in his life—as a student. Today he is serving as chairman or president of five corporations, including the worldwide Silva Mind Control International, Inc., which he founded.

He developed a new science for activating more of the mind, which he termed psychorientology, now accepted for inclusion in the dictionary. The Silva Method of Self Mind Control has been taught to millions of people in fifty-five countries around the world.

At the age of six, José Silva began to contribute to his own and his family's support, first by shining shoes and then adding newspaper sales. As a teenager, he organized a group of youngsters to sell products door-to-door. Before most other young adults had their first jobs, José had made money cleaning offices, selling baby chicks, reconditioning appliances, and "inventing" other ways to be of service.

During World War II he became interested in psychology, and later mind research, hypnosis, parapsychology, and biofeedback. He established an electronics technician training program at Laredo Junior College which was cited by VA officials as the best in Texas. He was a pioneer in the development of antenna systems in the early days of television.

As his electronics business grew, so did José Silva's research into subjective learning. For twenty-two years he worked on developing a mental training program and he launched it in 1966. The rest is a history of growth and expansion in the Silva Method throughout the world, acceptance by entire schools and businesses, and a continuing source of study and examination by world leaders in many fields as to its implications for the growth of mankind.

He is the author, with Philip Miele, of *The Silva Mind Control Method* published by Simon & Schuster in 1977 and a Psychology Today Book Club selection. He also authored the self-published *Reflections*.

On June 1, 1971, Governor Preston Smith of Texas commissioned José Silva an Ambassador of Good Will for the State of Texas. On February 24, 1977, José Silva was the "first personality to be publicly recognized" as Señor Internacional by the League of United Latin American Citizens (LULAC). On September 8, 1980, Governor Paul M. Calvo of Guam made José Silva an honorary Ambassador-at-Large for the territory of Guam. On September 3, 1980 the Guam legislature passed a resolution commending José Silva for the work he has done.

Robert B. Stone, Ph.D., is the author and coauthor of over sixty-five self-help books. He is a Silva Mind Control lecturer and has recently returned from a nine-month around-the-world lecture tour that included a score of countries on four continents. He teaches courses in using more of the mind at the University of Hawaii. He is a director of Hawaii's SCORE, the counseling arm of the U.S. Small Business Administration.

Acknowledgments

I wish to thank, in the order that they came to help, the following people: Dr. J.W. Hahn, Dr. N.E. West, Dord Fitz, Dr. Jeffrey Chang, Dr. Richard McKenzie, Harry F. McKnight, Dr. Frederick Bremner, Dr. George DeSau, Dr. Clancy D. McKenzie, and my associate on this project, Dr. Robert B. Stone, for his wisdom, expertise and great humanitarianism. All these people have made significant contributions to help make the Silva Mind Control Method the effective and successful program it is today.

Contents

3 How to Replace Manager Doldrums, Headaches, and Burnout with Dynamic Ongoing Enthusiasm · 51

4 How You Can Gain in Managerial Skills When You Control Your Mind · 67

5 The Silva Method for Getting More of Your Mind to Work for You · 86

6 Enhanced Memory and Concentration for Effective Management · 104

7 Silva Mind Control for a Successful Day • 119

8 Handling Difficult People and Solving Discipline Problems • 136

11 How to Make Your Presence More Effective at Meetings and in Other Situations · 192

12 Managing with Enhanced Perception in These Times of Change · 208

Index · 221

1

Common Manager Problems and How to Use the Silva Method for Solutions

A new dimension in human thinking has been discovered. It is now being used by business managers all over the world to improve their perception, their memory, their insight and their decision making. It is called the Silva Method. It is a method for getting in control of your mind, so that more of your mind goes to work for you.

When this happens, not only does your IQ go up, but subjective communication becomes possible. You are able to neutralize causes of low employee morale, reduce service complaints, lessen absenteeism, alleviate production bottlenecks, and presell.

The key is a relaxed level of thinking called Alpha. At Alpha, the intuitive right hemisphere of the brain is activated and functions more in balance with the logical left hemisphere.

We have gone about as far as we can go with the logical, deductive, intellectual processes of the left hemisphere. But education has largely ignored the intuitive, perceptive, creative faculties of the right hemisphere. Enter the Silva Method.

The theme of one of our recent Silva Method International conventions was "Innergize."

Modern man has been an outer man, influenced largely by forces outside of himself. Because these forces are often in conflict, man has been plagued by anger, frustration, and indecision.

Problems arise between individuals, families, groups, and nations. And man looks to these outer elements for solutions, often directing his anger at innocent parties.

The Silva Method manager is an outer man who is also able to be an inner man. The training has "innergized" him. He is able to control his inner—his attitudes and emotions—at the Alpha level. He becomes more "rational." Using the Alpha level of mind is what this training is all about. It is an inner, relaxed mental state.

Using the Alpha level, the Silva Method manager is able to be assertive and aggressive in an effective manner. He becomes a more successful manager, avoiding problems as well as solving them. His success becomes contagious and is reflected in the increased success of his colleagues and subordinates. (The manager of the future is just as likely to be a woman as a man, and I should say "him" or "her" throughout this book. Because it tends to become unwieldy, please accept "he" or "him" as referring to a person of either sex.)

The "innergized" man is able to function better as an outer man. He is drawing on an inner resource that the strictly outer man is deprived of.

This resource, as you now know, is the source of creativity and solutions. Please listen for a moment to Bette Taylor of Austin, Texas, as she tells you how she uses the Silva Method as a business manager.

PROGRAMMING FOR SOLUTIONS

"I am a business executive associated with several companies in Texas and Canada. It all came about by using Silva Mind Control, starting in line management. The first problem that any manager has, whether a supervisor, lead operator, or department head, is interaction with other people.

"The managers and the people they work with are going to be either hostile, indifferent, or bored, depending on their psychological patterns.

"I've worked with people in factory jobs for twenty years and have had to deal with people who were angry. When I took the Silva training, I was QCC supervisor at Motorola. Every day, at least twenty percent of my people were mad at me just because I walked in the door.

"I took a deep breath and as I exhaled I visualized a light around me. I saw it extending five or six feet around me. I programmed that everyone who came within that range would become more positive and more receptive to my working with them. It happened every time. I could see a person coming down the hall just 'loaded for bear,' his emotional guns blazing. As soon as he reached me, he would calm down. I could talk with him, reason with him. He would go away feeling better. He would react to my 'space' in a positive way.

"If we had a deadline to meet, I would go to the Alpha level and imagine everyone working as a team to meet it. And they did. I would see us doubling our quotas and reaching them. And we did. I would see myself being congratulated by my peers and getting promotions. And it would happen."

Seeing in this way at the Alpha level does to the human mind what programming does to a computer. Bette Taylor has programmed herself to earn a million dollars a year. And at this writing, she is well on her way to doing it.

A SOLUTION FOR EVERY PROBLEM

Every field or industry has its own problems. Every company in that field or industry has its special problems. And individuals in those companies have problems that are unique to them.

Outer, or objective (Beta), handling of these problems can employ many techniques, all with some relative success. Inner, or subjective (Alpha), handling of these problems can also employ a number of different techniques and each will be successful to some degree. More Alpha versus Beta as we proceed.

The Silva Method spells out specific techniques. Many are in this book. All have many applications.

Which technique you employ for a given problem is less important than it is that you do indeed employ a subjective technique in addition to objective techniques.

With the inner *and* the outer going for you, you are more

than doubling your management capability. Problems will dissolve in solutions.

The Silva Method techniques are only a beginning. You can vary them, combine them, and change them to fit special circumstances. You can invent your own ways to visualize and imagine at Alpha in order to straighten things out for everybody concerned.

You can write your own book.

Meanwhile, the best that the Silva Method can do for you is to provide you with a basic methodology. To do this we need to categorize problems in some general way.

In this chapter, the basic methodology will presume people problems. And we will divide such people problems into two main categories: Common everyday people problems, and unusual major people problems.

SOLVING ROUTINE PEOPLE PROBLEMS

Since you know you are going to run into common everyday problems, you can use the Silva Method now to program for future needs. I will describe the method to you in broad terms and then summarize more succinctly. Please remember this: the terms "going to level" and "programming" will be used in these instructions. How to go to level (Alpha) and how to program will be covered in future chapters.

To program for future needs, the clairvoyant executive goes to his level before falling asleep, and programs to awaken automatically at the proper time to program himself effectively for solving common, everyday problems.

When he awakens during the night, he again goes to his level. He then reviews in his mind that these problems arise from time to time and that to solve them expeditiously he needs to be at the correct dimension of mind. Some problems might require more left brain, others more right brain. (More about the functions of these two hemispheres later.) He then programs to be at the right state of mind by merely putting together the tips of the first three fingers of either hand. He says mentally, "Whenever I encounter this type of problem in the future, all I need to do is to bring together the tips of the first three fingers of either hand. By doing so, I will turn on my faculties. I will be extra-sensitive in perceiving information that I can use immediately to solve the problem." He then goes to sleep from his level.

Later, when the routine problem is encountered, the clairvoyant manager puts his three fingers together and enters a special state of mind wherein he becomes proficient in arriving at a proper decision for the benefit of all concerned. And this is so.

Summary

- At night, before falling asleep, close your eyes, turn them slightly upward and count yourself down to level.
- Program that you will awaken automatically at the best time to program yourself to solve routine problems.
- Fall asleep from level.
- When you awaken automatically, again go to level.
- Put the tips of the first three fingers together of either hand.
- State mentally, "This is all I need to do to turn on my faculties to solve routine problems. Whenever I bring together the tips of the first three fingers of either hand, I will be extra-sensitive in perceiving information that I can use to immediately solve such problems. And this is so."
- Fall asleep from level.
- When a problem arises, place the three fingers together as you address yourself to its solution.

SOLVING RARE, MAJOR PROBLEMS

To solve a special problem, or a problem that is of extra importance, the clairvoyant executive proceeds as before. That is, you program yourself at the Alpha level before falling asleep to awaken at the appropriate time to work on this special problem. When you awaken, you again go to the Alpha level, and program, using the Three Fingers Technique. In addition, you program that you will do the following:

You will take a minute or two during the day to go to level—in your office or in a private place—and you will program for a harmonious solution to the problem through subjective communication, and that this will contribute to a resolution of the problem. Subjective communication is a way of accomplishing mind-to-mind contact. How it is done will be detailed in the chapters ahead.

You then go to sleep from your Alpha level.

On the following day, or whenever the critical day arrives, go to your Alpha level for a few minutes in privacy, using the standard procedure that you use at night—the 3-to-1, 10-to-1 countdown, which will be given to you in later chapters. Once at your level, analyze the problem. What is involved? Who is involved? "Call in" the key person or persons involved, and "see" each in turn. Subjectively, in your imagination, discuss the problem. Get a feel for the person's position on the issue or issues.

Then, repeat to yourself that you are going to bring the tips of your three fingers together at the meeting, and this will cause you to use all of your sensing faculties to make the right selections and to say the right thing at the right time.

Then, you come out of your Alpha level and continue with your work. At the time of the meeting, put your three fingers together. Be confident that the right information will come to you, at the right time, to solve the problem so that everybody benefits.

A DEEP BREATH

If there is no time to go to your Alpha level prior to a confrontation on the problem, or if no specific event or meeting will occur relating to the problem, you can omit the subjective conversation and instead use an additional triggering technique.

Instead of preprogramming subjective communication prior to a meeting to help you solve the problem, preprogram that all you need to do is take a deep breath, hold it for a moment or two, and then let it out slowly. When you do this and put your three fingers together, you will turn on your subjective and objective sensing mechanisms to help you make the right decision, offer the proper suggestions, and say the right thing at the right time, so that everybody benefits by your input.

Summarizing the Procedure for Solving Special Problems

- At night, before falling asleep, close your eyes, turn them slightly upward and use the 3-to-1, 10-to-1 method to go to level.
- Program that you will awaken automatically at the appropriate time to program yourself to be able to solve the special problem.
- Fall asleep from level.
- When you awaken automatically, again go to level with the 3-to-1, 10-to-1 method.
- Put the tips of the first three fingers together of either hand and state mentally "Whenever I bring together the tips of the first three fingers of either hand, I turn on my faculties to solve this particular problem (identify problem)."
- Also state to yourself that before the meeting or event involving the problem, you will go to your level and have subjective communication with the key person or persons and that this will contribute to the resolution of the problem.
- Alternative: If there is no such meeting or event involved, instead of the above step, state to yourself that when you take a deep breath, hold it, and let it out slowly, with your three fingers together, your subjective and objective sensing mechanisms will be activated to enable you to handle the problem once and for all successfully for all concerned.
- Fall asleep from level.
- When the problem is about to be addressed at a meeting or event, seek privacy, go to your level, and hold a scene in your mind with the key person. Discuss the problem

in your imagination. See mutual understanding take place. Do the same with other persons involved.

• At the meeting or event, put your three fingers together, confident and expectant of a harmonious solution.

• (If no meeting or event is scheduled at the moment of the problem's manifestation, take a deep breath, hold it for a moment or two, let it out slowly, put your three fingers together, and again address yourself to the problem, confident and expectant of a harmonious solution.)

PROBLEM SOLVING: A TOP PRIORITY

I have a gut feeling that mankind's primary purpose on this planet is to solve problems. I will leave it to the philosophers to say whether this problem-solving purpose is so that we can learn and grow or whether it is to make this world a better place to live in. Regardless, when we are successful problem solvers, both take place.

Many business managers are conscientious about improving their knowledge and skill. Others, I am sorry to say, act as if life is a seventy-year coffee break. We need knowledge and information to solve problems. The more we have, the better problem solvers we are.

The most important skill we can acquire is the ability to instantly tap knowledge and information when we need it, and apply it to the problem at hand.

The Silva Method activates the brain to accomplish both of these steps. It activates both hemispheres of the brain so as to either recall needed information learned or sense information needed but not learned; and then to apply it to a solution.

Theoretically speaking, the Silva Method could be a vast equalizer: Every manager, no matter how educated, skilled, or experienced, can sense the needed information to solve any problem. This could indicate that a manager who does not attend special seminars or read up on latest developments will succeed as a problem solver anyhow.

Not so. The manager who coasts along this way is not expressing desire, expectation, and belief, so necessary to the activation of brain neurons. In fact, the "coffee break" attitude towards a job can indeed lull brain neurons into inactivity.

The Silva Method works for everybody, as long as there is desire, expectancy, and belief. It is not the ticket to a seventy-year coffee break.

LEARNING AND PROBLEM SOLVING

I have never been idle in my life. I enjoy my family and I enjoy socializing. I, of course, enjoy working. What I do not enjoy doing is wasting time.

I get up at 5:00 A.M. to start work. No matter where I go, I have a book in my hand. Is it a novel? I have never read a novel in my life. I am not saying that you should be like me. Read novels, if you enjoy novels, but also read to learn. Is it a comic book? The only time I ever read a comic book was when I taught myself the English language.

The book I have with me all day is a text or a lesson or an instructional book of some sort. It is a book that has something constructive in it.

The more a business manager stays on top of things in his field objectively (reading and studying), the better he is able to function subjectively (through intuition, perception, and clairvoyance).

Nothing in this book is intended to circumvent objective methods. Everything in this book is intended to help you add subjective methods to your objective methods in order to become a bicameral manager—a manager who uses both hemispheres of his brain.

Keep pursuing knowledge. Encourage colleagues and subordinates to do likewise. The more successful problem solvers there are in the world, the better world this will be.

MANAGERIAL GROWTH

Several months after taking the Silva Method training, Mrs. Kitt Curtis of Calabasas, California, her daughter Geri, and a third woman, Betty Ash, decided to solve a problem in the coffee business. They started the Curtis Coffee Co., Inc., roasting, blending and packaging "a higher quality product at more competitive prices." They became the only women in the world with their own coffee roasting plant. The growth of this company led to a spinoff of another company providing coffee service to business.

Another graduate of the Silva Method, June Brooks of Ardmore, Oklahoma, became the only woman "wildcatter" in the oil business. She went on to lead a campaign for decontrol, speaking to groups all over the country on how that would be a beneficial solution for all concerned.

Men and women who train themselves to use more of their minds and then direct their energy to solving problems grow in many ways. Professionally, that growth is not confined to their own companies. They frequently get recognition by the trade association, the chamber of commerce, a professional society or other such agencies.

The leaders of society and business are the problem solvers. And they frequently become leaders in their cities, states, and in the nation.

Objective and subjective approaches, working together toward solving problems, are an unbeatable team. We were created by nature to solve problems subjectively and objectively but, somewhere along the way, we lost the subjective approach.

Now we run the risk of having the pendulum swing too far in the subjective dimension. As people in all walks of life, including business executives, see the quick and easy results obtained through subjective functioning, they can easily go overboard and use subjective techniques more and more at the expense of usual objective techniques.

This would be as much a mistake as before, when only objective techniques were used. We need to have a balance. We need to use both the objective and the subjective approaches to problem solving.

Our subjective functioning permits us to tap ideas and solutions in the creative or causal realm. We become a "cause." Our objective functioning permits us to implement those ideas and solutions in the realm of effect. We have an effect. The subjective person, unable to function objectively, is ineffective. The objective person, unable to function subjectively, is a creature of circumstances.

The subjective-objective person is an effective creator of circumstances.

It is little wonder that some companies now make the Silva Method an initial step after employment.

RECURRING PROBLEMS WITH A SPECIFIC PERSON

The objective person can frequently be objectionable. He is out of touch with the common good and functions strictly for his own good. If you have such a person in your organization, he can be a source of friction, personality clashes, discipline infractions, and other recurring problems.

Just as you combine subjective communication plus a triggering device (three fingers together) to solve problems of a more general nature, you can combine these two techniques to take care of a problem individual.

Let us say, for example, that one of your employees is an avid newspaper reader. His reading of the newspaper while on the job has demoralizing effects on other employees, on customers or clients, and on his own job productivity. No amount of talk has done any good. He still keeps the morning paper with him until lunch, and the afternoon paper the rest of the day.

Since objective means have proved to be of no avail, you need to add subjective means to your efforts. Here is how.

Go to your level at night and program to awake at the best time to program this problem person, whom we shall call Mr. Read. The correct time will be when Mr. Read's brain waves are receptive to your subjective communication. When you wake up automatically, go to your level again and imagine you are talking to Mr. Read. The picture is directly in front of you. Explain that you understand his interest in the news, that it is good to keep abreast of world developments, but that it interferes with company morale and production.

Move the picture slightly to the left and see Mr. Read, newspaper in hand, drinking coffee or water or whatever liquid refreshment you know Mr. Read takes. As he drinks, you see him put the newspaper away. His drink now triggers the "put away newspaper" reaction. Move the picture slightly to the left again. Now Mr. Read is working without a newspaper. The problem is solved. Feel relief. Go to sleep from level.

Your brain neurons are in touch with Mr. Read's brain neurons when you are at the Alpha level. Your higher nature is appealing to his higher nature, bypassing his critical consciousness. This is quite different from the supervisor's criticizing an employee. Now the message gets through.

The triggering device you have visualized, Mr. Read's drink, is now an aid to Mr. Read. You have given him a new programming to take the place of the old programming that he no longer wants. He can be willing to stop reading on the job, but he is in the habit of reading on the job. Now, every time he takes a drink of liquid—such as water or coffee or tea, which he is accustomed to drinking on the job—that drink triggers a desire to discard the paper on the job.

Watch it work. Help it to work even better, by reinforcing this procedure for several nights.

Summary

- Go to level and program to awaken at the appropriate time to program for the solution to this problem with a special person.

- When you awake automatically, again go to your level and have an understanding but convincing discussion with this person toward the elimination of the problem for the good of all concerned.

- Now see the problem person manifesting the problem. Move the picture slightly to the left and see him drinking a liquid that you know he drinks frequently. As he drinks, he is reminded about the need to correct the problem.

- Move the scene again slightly to the left. See him working with no sign of the problem. Feel it. Know it to be so. Fall asleep from level.

- Reinforce on successive nights.

PROGRAMMING WITH EYES OPEN

When you have programmed at night repeatedly with successful results, you can preprogram at night and then program in the daytime. This is done with the eyes open in the following way:

Let us say, for example, that we have a worker who is in a slump. He is not producing at the level that you and he both know he can produce, but no apparent cause can be isolated.

To preprogram at night, program to wake up at the right time. Once awake, go to level, and tell yourself that to correct this problem, the next time the problem is apparent, all you have to do is put your three fingers together, unfocus your eyes, and see three pictures. In the first picture, the problem worker is lax on the job. In the second picture, slightly to the left, the problem worker is drinking his favorite fluid and is being reminded of the need to step up his work effectiveness. In the third picture, the problem worker is no longer a problem. He is working at top performance, better than you or he even thought possible.

With this method, once preprogrammed at Alpha at night, there is no need to go to level during the day. The act of putting together the tips of the first three fingers of either hand, unfocusing the eyes, and daydreaming the three scenes will activate your right brain and you will be functioning with objective and subjective faculties. You will be helping to solve the problem.

Fred S., manager of a supermarket, used this method on a checkout clerk who was not only slowing up but beginning to hit the wrong keys. Putting him in stock control for a few days did not help. The Silva Method did. His speed and accuracy improved. Fred later made him assistant manager.

Summary

- Program to wake up at the right time.
- When awake, return to level, and program that you can improve the level of the person's work quality by putting

your three fingers together, unfocusing your eyes, and seeing three scenes: the problem scene, the fluid drinking scene to the left (the fluid will remind him of his need to heighten work quality), and still further to the left, the work going splendidly.

• Fall asleep from level.

• Whenever confronted by the problem, put your three fingers together, unfocus your eyes, and see the three scenes as before.

• The final scene—of the work going well—will become the reality. And this is so.

PROBLEM-SOLVING ALTERNATIVES REVIEWED

1. Preprogramming the Three Fingers Technique and then using it at the moment of the problem. (For routine problems.)

2. The Three Fingers Technique plus subjective conversation prior to confrontation. (For a special problem with confrontation or meeting.)

3. Preprogramming the Three Fingers Technique plus deep breath, a technique that you will learn in the pages ahead. (For special problem with no prior meeting or confrontation.)

4. Preprogramming subjective communication as the drinking of coffee, water, etc. as a triggering device. (For recurring problems with a particular person.)

As stated earlier, there are many ways of thinking at the Beta level and, likewise, there are many ways of thinking at the Alpha level. There is no one correct objective approach and no one correct subjective approach.

We are going to close this chapter with several Case Studies similar to those that will be presented later in Chapter 8 largely on discipline problems. At the end of these Case Studies, we will provide the recommended solution, #1, #2, #3, or #4, as listed here. If you decide to use a different approach, it does not mean you will not be successful. Your route will get you there, too. Variations on solutions are not critical and may indeed be based on personal likes or dislikes rather than on any factual principle.

The only way you can really err on these Case Studies is to decide to ignore all four subjective approaches and stick to the "tried and true" objective approaches. Subjective approaches have also been tried, and have been found "true." Problems, by definition, are situations that continue to exist despite objective attempts to solve them. So, subjective approaches—tried and true—are the answer.

CUTTING DOWN ON OVERTIME

Case Study I. Arthur S. is a press foreman in a large printing plant. It is company policy that overtime hours are to be authorized by you the supervisor, with an automatic exception where a delivery has to be met the next day and production lagged in the final hours of the day before such overtime authorization could be issued by you.

However, Arthur S. has been working overtime almost daily. He is a senior employee, and has been with the firm a long time before the establishment of a company policy on overtime, and before the union-management relationship placed hours worked under close scrutiny and control.

You have spoken repeatedly to Arthur S. about his overtime. His classic answer has been, "I needed to straighten up and ready things for the next day. Don't worry about it, Boss."

But you must worry about it. You are under instructions to adhere strictly to company policy and also to cut down on expensive overtime. Arthur S. must turn in overtime vouchers if he punches out late. You must honor them. You cannot throw Arthur S. out of the plant bodily at closing time; nor can you discharge this conscientious man. What do you do?

HANDLING SEXUAL HARASSMENT

Case Study II. Frank G., about forty, married, with three children, is an outgoing, good-humored, star salesman. He is always kidding others to get laughs. But you have now received two complaints from women—one a salesperson, the other an office worker. Both said that Frank G. has been "busy with his hands."

"I tried to laugh him off," said the saleswoman, "but when he persisted I had to slap him."

"He took me by surprise," said the typist. "He was standing behind me, explaining the contract changes, when all of a sudden he grabbed me."

You spoke with Frank G. after the first incident and he roared with laughter. This took you by surprise and you did not pursue the matter at the time. Now, with this second complaint, you cannot let the matter ride. What do you do?

DEALING WITH THE COMMUNITY

Case Study III. You are the head of a cement plant located near the harbor of a small New England town. You have sand digging rights in a hillside about three miles inland. To transport the sand to your plant, trucks must pass through a residential area. There have been incidents of excessive speed. You have reprimanded the drivers. But the complaints continue to come in. Three parent-teacher organizations have held a joint meeting. A representative of your firm, who happens to be a parent in that area, has attended and reported the proceedings to you. It was a hostile meeting. They have decided to send a delegation of three parents to see you. You have agreed to meet with them. The meeting is set for tomorrow. What do you do?

APPLYING THE SILVA METHOD
IN CASE I

Suggested Technique. It is recommended that #4 be used. Arthur S. is a coffee drinker. You can program him to begin his cleanup and preparation time earlier and earlier. You program at level that Arthur S. understands the overtime problem more every time he drinks coffee. See him responding by beginning his preparations for the next day before closing time instead of after.

Alternate Techniques. You can reinforce the above by preprogramming that a special word or phrase, used objectively in the normal course of conversation by you in Arthur S.'s presence will trigger earlier cleanup and preparation. Other techniques provided in this or following chapters will also work, but some, like merely visualizing the problem solved, would be asking a boy to do a man's work.

APPLYING THE SILVA METHOD IN CASE II

Suggested Technique. It is recommended that #2 be used. Set up a meeting with Frank G. in one or two days. Meanwhile, preprogram the Three Fingers Technique and also have a subjective conversation with Frank G. on the matter. Explain the problems that his sexual conduct is causing in the company. Remind him that it can lead to assault charges by a complainant and hurt both the company and his family. Ask him to find more socially acceptable outlets for his youthful exuberance. Before the meeting, go to level in your office and repeat this subjective conversation. At the meeting put your three fingers together.

Alternative Techniques. Again, other techniques will help but may not be focused enough to bring an end to Frank G.'s office behavior. A possible additional step could be to invite an expert into your subjective conversation scene. This expert could be a minister, a psychologist, or any person whom Frank G. respects. Ask this expert what approach in your imaginary conversation with Frank G. would be most productive. The methodology is provided in the chapters ahead.

APPLYING THE SILVA METHOD IN CASE III

Suggested Technique. It is recommended that #2 be used, supplemented by #3. Again, this is an important meeting situation where preprogramming the Three Fingers Technique plus conducting a subjective conversation with the principals will pave the way for a mutually satisfying solution. You might call in a public relations consultant to participate in the subjective conversations, if you would feel more confident or comfortable with such assistance. Ideas will come to you during this subjective event. Remember them and act on them. You might see additional employees at the meeting whom you had not planned on including. Invite them. They may be residents of that community also, or they may provide problem-solving ideas. You might see the problem ended in two years when the sand supply in that area is exhausted and a park will be built for the community in its place. Consider all subjective communications as two-way streets. You are not only communicating your position on a top level basis, but the thoughts and matters that arise in your imagination can be clues to accommodating solutions. The deep breath technique (#3) can be useful during informal conversations with the community representatives prior to the formal start of the meeting and following.

Alternate Techniques. See the problem to the right (past). See the meeting straight ahead (present). See everybody satisfied, slightly to the left (future), and trucks moving carefully with no children in view, more to the left.

THE SCOPE OF SUBJECTIVE COMMUNICATIONS

As you use subjective communications in your pre-programming and programming, you begin to accept the fact that your mind is in touch with other minds.

This acceptance improves the flow. As resistance is lowered, current flow increases. You are able to use subjective communications in more and more situations.

Bette Taylor, whom we quoted earlier in this chapter, went into a business project with Dr. J.W. Hahn, a Silva Method lecturer and our science consultant. The Hahn-Taylor Trading Company went into business in January, 1982. Their first problem was to locate people with specific products or skills. They used the Silva Method to communicate subjectively with whomever they were seeking. Within several months they had established an international network of people who needed one another to buy or to sell and were netting a high volume of finder's fees.

I am not suggesting that you eliminate interoffice memos, the United States Postal Service, or Western Union. But the scope of subjective communications is so limitless, the delivery so fast and accurate, and the price so right, I am going to expand on this valuable procedure in the next chapter and some later chapters.

2

Triggering Creative Ideas to Stay Ahead of the Competition

The mind is creative.

Man has created vehicles for rapid transportation, buildings that reach for the sky, means for electronic communication, artistic and scientific wonders. All of these creations have involved man's hands and machines, but primarily they involved his mind.

Nothing that exists in our civilized world would be here if it did not first exist as an image in somebody's mind. Only from such an image can there emerge a sketch, a shop drawing, a pattern, a diagram, a formula, a mold, or a blueprint.

What is the source of creativity?

That is the eternal question. Fortunately, we do not have to know the answer to tap into that source. The mind is a channel for it. All we have to do is *permit* the mind to tap that source, so that the creative idea can be brought from the recesses of the vast unconscious (right brain) to the sensory conscious (left brain).

This happens at ten cycles per second of brain wave frequency. Alpha is the center of the brain's frequency span. This is the frequency at which the brain is centered and at which both hemispheres work in concert.

Concerted action by both hemispheres creates solutions to problems. Our brain becomes a bridge from "there" to "here." We know a lot about "here," but we can only theorize about "there." Whatever or wherever "there" is, it abounds in creative solutions.

In this chapter, we will learn how to apply the Silva Method for enhanced perception of these creative solutions. By going to the alpha level, the clairvoyant executive activates his perception of what other executives—with one-half of their brains relatively inactive—can only dimly perceive, if at all.

NECESSITY AND INVENTION

One of the first persons to use the Silva Method for inventive purposes was my brother Juan Silva. He was working on a mechanical vending machine for Mexico back in 1958, some ten years before we ended our basic research and began to offer the Mind Control training publicly.

I will let him relate to you how he used his Alpha level and how the results unfolded. But keep in mind that, in the quarter century since then, we have evolved more elaborate mental means to use the Alpha level for creative projects. These, too, will also be provided in this chapter. Now here is Juan's story:

"Faced with the need to create a mechanism that would handle any combination of Mexican coins to activate the vending device, I would go to level each night after going to bed. I would then repeat the goal mentally, the device I needed to invent, and the importance of achieving this goal. By going to level and programming in this way, I was reinforcing my desire, boosting it. By doing this just before going to sleep, I was exciting my imagination and activating my dreams.

"I knew I was getting somewhere because I began to have dreams about nuts and bolts and machine parts. But these dreams did not seem to make any sense. During the day I also felt some results. I found myself spending longer hours at the drawing board. But still the answers eluded me. I had a gut feeling that I should be doing something that I was not doing.

"One day, my stepfather, seeing my frustration, suggested I work at a lathe. 'Your hands will know what to do,' he said. I took his advice. In a way, I thought then that this was outside the Mind Control method. But today I realize that, when you program for answers to come, these answers can come through other people, too.

"When I went to work on the lathe, and did something, that something led to something else. It was a better method than working on paper and asking the brain to understand gear ratios, transmission speeds, and all of the other mechanical notions.

"As I began to work on the lathe, I found that I was using the lathe as a gear. It is not supposed to be used as a gear. It moves too fast. It is the wrong shape. But as I worked with it as a gear, I began to see the application of an elongated gear—a lineal gear. This became the primary part in the converter, the unit that enabled the coins to be released mechanically.

"This breakthrough was a lesson to me. Because we are mind and body, we have to involve our body as part of the creative process. We need to move, perform, do. It was when I involved my body that my mind was able to show my hands what to do.

"My completed mechanical vending machine incorporated characteristics that eventually proved critical but which I had no prior concern about. My unit was a multiple priced vendor. Each product could be sold at a different price. Not only that but four different coins could be used in any combination to total the price. This was beyond the existing coinage. Six months later, when Mexico coined new denominations, the machine was ready for them!

"Could I have done it without Mind Control? Perhaps. Even without the Mind Control method, I would have been using the same basics but in a rudimentary way. The Silva Method accelerated and enhanced the end product. Of this, I am sure."

My brother Juan continued to use the Silva Method when he was engaged to put the vending machine into production. The prototype was used to establish a production line involving the appropriate tools and equipment under his supervision. Once the factory was tooled up and began production, Juan was prevailed upon to stay and manage the factory. Within a few months he had increased production from 23 units a month to 150 units a month. But now he was programming in a different way.

GROUP INVENTIVENESS

"I continued to program myself before going to sleep. I began to make more sense out of my dreams; they were telling me things. I could feel the difference in the morning. I felt better; I was more alert; my imagination was more active. I had programmed for reaching specific goals by enhancing my desire to attain those goals, and I had an inner confidence that it was happening.

"But I also began to involve other people. When I programmed to reach a solution, I first visualized the problem, including the people involved in the problem. Then, when I imagined the solution—not a specific solution, but no more problem—I also imagined people who could provide the solution entering the picture.

"That is exactly what happened. We moved from having to import most of our prefabricated parts to being able to use domestic sources. They showed up.

"I moved even further in involving other people in my nightly programming. I programmed for the solution to specific problems to benefit all of the employees in the factory. It was not only my problem as manager. It was their problem. They needed to become part of the solution and to be properly compensated for that.

"By opening the vistas of my programming in this way, I found even better results. I visualized symbolically all 478 employees and the administrators. I saw them working for the common good and participating in the common good. I did not want to 'hog' everything. It is to this 'common good' programming that I attribute the vast strides we made in production and competitive advantage."

This sounds idealistic, but creating for the common good is actually selfish. As the company benefits, you benefit.

"But how do I get credit for it?" you might ask.

Personal glory is not a valid Silva Method goal. If you program for ego satisfaction, you might wind up getting the personal credit. But we prefer to go for the cash. As the company profits, we all profit.

BUSINESS AWAKES

This book may provide your first exposure to ways of enhancing perception and clairvoyance. But you will be hearing more and more about the intuitive faculties and right brain activation in the business press with every passing day.

Nobel Prize winner (1981) Roger Sperry of Cal Tech, who contributed much to left brain, right brain understanding, said that our educational system, as well as science in general, tends to neglect the nonverbal form of intellect and that it seems modern society discriminates against the right hemisphere.

Writing in the April 1982 issue of *AMA Management Digest,* Michael Burnson suggests that one way to thoroughly understand a business situation with the help of the right hemisphere is to draw or diagram the situation. This requires imaging, he reminds us, a skill neglected by our schooling, but one which helps to shift us into what he calls the R-mode, or intuitive right brain functioning.

Businessmen are awakening to this new intuitive mode. This used to be the scene: Nobody was permitted to leave the meeting until the problem was solved. Meals were brought in. Tension mounted. The stress cut off creativity. Possibly eight to ten hours later, the meeting ended with failure.

Today, this is more likely to be the scene: All personnel are invited to take ten minutes on arriving in the morning to relax and fantasize about a perfect day. A similar period is recommended after lunch. There is no tension, no forcing, no failure.

Burnson lists a few things that managers can do to shift to intuitive modes of functioning, such as deep muscle relaxation, daydreaming, doodling, or turning on some music. These are all good, but we need to understand what we are doing when we relax and when we daydream. We are going to the Alpha level. Understanding this process brings creativity and intuition under control. We do not have to depend on that flash of insight that may or may not come. We become able to control our insight.

Writing in the same publication, under the title "A Whole-Brained Approach to Futuristic Management," Frank Feather and Gayle Hudgens spell out five steps in the creative process:

1. *Preparation.* The left brain does its homework.

2. *Absorption.* The right brain images the groundwork and the goal.

3. *Incubation.* A period of gestation and maturation of ideas that takes place at the subconscious level.

4. *Illumination.* The "Eureka!" factor. The idea explodes into our conscious when we least expect it.

5. *Verification.* A logical left brain process that eliminates extraneous ideas and checks the final conclusion.

To me, these steps are certainly basic, what you might call the anatomy of the brain's creative process. What I am more interested in is getting this creative process under control.

I am going to devote the rest of this chapter to a detailed how-to procedure for obtaining solutions to creative problems. You have a built-in generator. Here is how to turn it on.

ACTIVATING YOUR IDEA GENERATOR

First, let us assume that the business manager is associated with a firm that is not the leader in its field. This firm needs to keep coming up with creative ideas to improve its competitive position. Later, we will approach it from the number one position.

The business manager in a firm which is striving to better its position in the field should proceed as follows. I will discuss the procedure as I go along and will then summarize it more succinctly.

Go to your level before falling asleep at night, by closing your eyes, turning them slightly upwards and then counting from 3 to 1, and from 10 to 1. (There is a training you must give yourself for this to be effective, as provided in Chapter 4.) At level, tell yourself mentally, "I will awake automatically tonight at the best time to program for creative ideas, to contend better with the competition and to move up toward the top." Add any specifics about those ideas that bring them to bear more directly on the firm and its situation. Fall asleep from level.

When you awaken during the night, again go to level with the 3-to-1, 10-to-1 method. Then select somebody you know who is at the top or near the top in your field. Make a "copy" of that individual and visualize that replica in the picture with you, at your side. He will answer your questions as an expert consultant. Here is how this is done.

Tell your expert what you plan to do. Test your ideas. Pause and give your expert a chance to answer. Do this by taking your mind off the matter. Disconnect. Then once again address yourself to the project. "What is it I must do to get ahead of competition?" What comes to mind is the expert's opinion.

If several ideas come to you, use the elimination process. Number them. Compare idea number one with idea number two. Then ask your expert which is best. Stop thinking about it for a fraction of a second, disconnecting yourself. Then resume thinking about which is best and the answer that comes will be the right one. If there is a third option, compare the answer just received, say number two, with number three. Again, ask your expert, disconnect, and resume thinking about which is best. The number that pops into your mind is then the best of the three options.

In effect, you are attuning your brain neurons with those of an expert in the field. You have picked the top man in the field as your expert. This is his advice.

When you put this advice into practice and see that it has indeed created a better competitive position for you, continue to use this process as a regular programming event. Every few days, go to your level before falling asleep and repeat the process: program to awake automatically; when you do, go to level again and review your success; thank the system, including special thanks to the expert, and again ask for creative ideas to compete better.

Repetition makes you more and more skilled at this, by reinforcing success. Sometimes there are good aspects to a creative step you have come up with and also some aspects that are not so good. Avoid thinking in terms of the aspects that are not so good. Dwell instead on the successful aspects. In this way, you will set the stage for more success.

STAYING NUMBER ONE

If you are the leading company in your field, and you want to stay number one, you have to bring in creative ideas as an ongoing process. In order to do this, you need to follow the same basic procedure as before, but now you are the leader in the field. So a different process is followed in selecting the expert whom you can question at your level.

Instead of one expert, you select several. You must know who the key managers are in the most competitive firms. These are the people who will answer your questions. These are the people whose "copies" will be in your nighttime scene.

Let us say there are three major companies keeping your company on its collective toes. Who is the person in each firm charged with creative leadership? You need to know his name and what he looks like. If there is a second man with these responsibilities, who is he and what does he look like?

Armed with this information, you are ready to proceed.

After going to bed at night, and just before falling asleep, go to level and program, as before, to awake at the right time to work on this project. Fall asleep from your level. When you awake automatically, go to level again. Visualize the experts. Select one expert and ask him the question, "What new idea needs to be implemented in the industry?" You can use different words to fit your business situation. The thrust is to request a creative idea of a timely and practical nature.

Once you ask the question, disconnect yourself momentarily, then again begin to think about the answer. The idea that comes is the answer from person number one. As you begin again to think about the answer to your question, something will enter your mind. It will feel as though you are making it up, or as though you are guessing. This is the right feeling.

You are now ready to do the same with expert number two and expert number three.

When you have obtained ideas in this manner from all three experts, you should review these ideas in your mind. Compare one with the other. Which idea seems to be right for your company? Which fits best into your present marketing plans? Which can you implement the fastest?

The answers to these and similar questions will serve to screen the three or more ideas that have come to mind by way of the experts. One will emerge as the natural one for you to pursue. Or, possibly, a new idea will emerge from this thinking which combines some attributes of two or more of these ideas. If it is not obvious which idea is best for your company, use the elimination method that will be explained later.

Fix the decision in your mind, thank your experts, and go to sleep from your level.

Reviewing and Condensing

- Go to level and program to awake at the right time to work on this project.
- When you awake automatically, enter your level again.

To Reach the Top	To Stay at the Top
• Make a visual copy of the person at the head of the industry. Ask him for competitive ideas.	• Make visual copies of the key persons in the most competitive firms. Ask each for competitive ideas.

- Disconnect after each query. When you begin again to think about the problem, the answer that comes is your expert's.

• Use the elimination process to arrive at the best creative idea.	• Compare the ideas to select the best for your firm or to synthesize from them what is best for your firm. If in doubt, use the elimination method.

- Thank your expert(s) and fall asleep from level.

TIPS FOR CLAIRVOYANT CREATIVITY

When you awake in the morning, after a creative session such as the one just described, write down all of the ideas that emerged, not just the one that was selected.

The subordinate ideas may become valuable in the days or weeks ahead.

No matter how unusual an idea is, accept it as a legitimate creative thought. If you laugh at yourself (or at the copy of an expert you have created), you discourage the flow of ideas.

Do not judge. Do not jump in with a "silly" or "won't work." This is the left brain's jealous logic trying to upstage the right brain's sometimes naive, but more often than not, valuable approach.

Respect all ideas that come to you at your level in response to your queries to experts or in response to your elimination method queries. Trust your Alpha functioning.

Do not discuss this process with colleagues unless they, too, are training their perceptive abilities with the Silva Method. Such discussions are nonproductive. You would be offering the creative product of your total brain along with the product of a person using less than half of his.

Discuss your clairvoyant idea (not the process through which it was obtained) with the company personnel whose responsibility it is to make the decision to go ahead and to then implement that decision.

It would be helpful first to do some additional programming.

1. Program for the creative idea to be understood and well received by using subjective communication at your level.

2. Once accepted for implementation, program for the creative project to be successful, by using scenes of progress progressively to the left.

Do not let this be a one-time event. Million dollar ideas are a dime a dozen at the creative level. They are waiting to be fished out of the great unconscious and put to use. Continue to use your experts at night to help you create better and better products and services for your company.

CREATIVE DREAMS

My brother Juan mentioned earlier in this chapter how, in the process of activating his creative imagination, his dreams become more active.

Dreams are a source of creative ideas. Mankind has been benefiting from information received in dreams for centuries.

Back in 1869, a Russian scientist Dmitri Mendeleev had been trying unsuccessfully to create a way of categorizing the elements based on their atomic weights. One night the Periodic Table of the Elements appeared to him in a dream. He wrote it down immediately on awakening in the morning. He had to make only one small correction in it.

Elias Howe had been working on a lock-stitch sewing machine. He could not get the needle to work. Then one night he had a dream about being attacked by natives with spears. In the point of each spear was a hole. When he awoke, he realized that this could be the answer. He had never tried putting the hole of the needle near the point. It worked. This became the Singer sewing machine.

Niels Bohr received the atomic theory in a dream. Many other scientists have had their successful theories come to them in the content of a dream.

When we dream, the brain cycles increase. We move up from Delta, just a few cycles per second, to Alpha or ten cycles per second. It is the same level of mind that you are able to enter and be creative at while awake. It can be entered from either direction—asleep or awake.

Awake, you now have Alpha under your control. You can enter it at will and use it for any purpose you desire. Asleep, it is less under your control. You enter it automatically every one and a half hours, and stay in it for ten to fifteen minutes while you dream. As you work more with Alpha while you are awake, it works more for you while you are asleep. Dreams become more pertinent to your problems, more meaningful to your goals.

It is recommended that you acquire the habit of writing

down your dreams on awakening at night or in the morning. Keep writing materials handy and perhaps a small flashlight if you do not want to disturb a bedmate. The more you write about a dream, immediately on awakening, the more details you will remember. On the other hand, if you do not write down a dream immediately on awakening, it will all slip away.

Dreams frequently offer important messages concerning solutions to our problems and concerning our attitudes and emotions that might need to be better handled or controlled for reduced stress and increased health.

When I needed additional funds to complete the research for this training, I programmed to have a dream that would help with that problem. That night I dreamt of a five-digit number. I wrote it down. Later that day I saw the number on a Mexican lottery ticket. I bought it and won exactly the amount of money I needed.

Our logical left brain gives up at such a happening; our clairvoyant right brain takes it in stride.

THE SOURCE OF CREATIVITY

The more research we do into left and right brain hemisphere functioning, the more we are beginning to understand the creative process.

Standard creative approaches are largely left brain. The "think tanks" are left brain. "Brainstorming" is left brain. The textbook references to methodologies for convergent, divergent, deductive, and analytical thinking do not take into consideration the flash of insight, the "Eureka!" or the "Aha!".

Because the right brain appears to be our connection to a vast unconscious intelligence in the universe, and because this right brain begins to function on a par with the left brain at the Alpha level, it appears that at the Alpha level we are "hooked in" to this vast intelligence.

Research in physics is leading us to a similar conclusion. The western view of the universe has been as separate galaxies, separate solar systems, separate planets, separate organisms, separate objects. However, physicists are beginning to see a subatomic world. It is a world of energy, interdependent and interrelated, and in a state of constant change.

Fritjof Capra, physicist at the University of California at Berkeley and author of *The Tao of Physics*, states, "The basic oneness of the universe is not only the central characteristic of the mystical experience, but is also one of the most important revelations of modern physics."

If modern physics has indeed revealed that we are not as separate as we think we are, then modern physics has also revealed the source of creative ideas. It must be from the "basic oneness." There is no other place.

I call this oneness higher intelligence. But because it fits religious concepts, it deserves to be capitalized. So when I refer to tuning in to Higher Intelligence, you know I am not referring to something outside of ourselves but rather to the oneness of which we are part and which we are able to tap when the two hemispheres of our brain are unified—at the Alpha level.

Higher Intelligence is the source of creation as we see it today and the ongoing source of creativity.

HOW IMAGINARY EXPERTS ASSIST US

It may seem peculiar, even weird, to some managers that part of the Silva Method is the mental imaging of experts in the field to answer our questions.

Are we tapping their brains? Are we stealing their secrets? Are we doing something unethical, like invading their privacy?

To understand what is really happening, we need to focus on the concept of oneness. We need to be able to accept this concept, not just intellectually—and for us westerners that is hard enough—but also through feeling it. And for us competitive westerners that is even more difficult.

I say it is more difficult for westerners because we traditionally perceive the world as objects and events existing separately in space and time. We have a personal consciousness.

In the East, consciousness is transpersonal. It sees the

oneness behind the separateness. Eastern philosophy transcends the separateness of time and space.

We dismiss this in the West as a delusion, a mystical experience, signifying nothing.

In the East, they dismiss our personal concept as delusional and illusory.

Now research in the field of physics and of the brain is pointing to a rightful place in man's consciousness for both concepts.

There is a need for man's logical and reasoning faculties which deal with the problems of the separateness. And there is a need for man's intuitive, perceptive, and clairvoyant faculties which draw solutions from the oneness.

You might say that this is lower intelligence (man) funneling into this material world of effect the wisdom of Higher Intelligence from the nonmaterial world of cause.

This is pretty "heavy," I agree. And earlier I agreed that we did not have to understand how clairvoyance worked in order to use it. This is still true. But maybe you are now beginning to see the purpose of creating experts, or consultants, while you are at level.

We have found this to be an acceptable Western way of transcending the separateness. After all, if we can invite into our mental space anybody we wish to help solve our problems, we are drawing on the family of man.

EAST MEETS WEST

The Silva Method is being increasingly used in countries of the eastern world. I am of the West. The reaction of eastern people to this western approach is interesting to me. Several years ago, my writing associate, Dr. Stone, went to Tokyo at the invitation of the Silva Method coordinator there, Bill M. Sasaki, to introduce the training in English with simultaneous Japanese translation. Here is an interesting aspect of his experience.

"The class included university staff, media people, some businessmen, and one or two religious leaders. I was careful to avoid possible cultural conflicts and so stayed strictly with the scientific principles involved with little to no references to spiritual implications.

"After the training was completed, the graduates arranged a banquet to celebrate. Everybody got up in turn to make a speech. My simultaneous translator was now working in reverse, converting their Japanese into English for me to understand.

"I was amazed. Each graduate extolled the training from a spiritual viewpoint. They felt enlightened, illuminated, closer to Divinity. Not one scientific word was uttered. They were describing a mystical experience, and in the process alluding to me as a mentor and to José Silva as even higher than that."

Although there usually is not a reaction such as this in the West, there is an unmistakable euphoria at graduations. Individuals young and old feel an exhilaration at being able to function demonstrably as clairvoyants. It is a transcendent experience. It transcends our conventional Western sense of separateness and of time and space limitations.

This is a time in history when the spiritual East is becoming more material. And the material West is becoming more meditative. Maybe the twain shall meet. Maybe the right brained East and left brained West are meeting at the center—at Alpha.

As Dr. Stone puts it:

"Here in Hawaii, where East meets West, our word for the feeling of oneness or togetherness is Aloha. Just put a handle on the 'o' for oneness and you get Alpha."

Alpha is a handle on creativity—wherever it comes from.

3

How to Replace Manager Doldrums, Headaches, and Burnout with Dynamic Ongoing Enthusiasm

The clairvoyant executive can use the subjective dimension to correct objective problems. The subjective dimension means a mental dimension where the mind functions through visualization and imagination.

The importance of the subjective dimension has only recently been appreciated. Up until the past generation, the objective dimension has eclipsed the subjective dimension. The physical reality has upstaged the nonphysical and labeled it nonreal.

We now know otherwise. Thanks to biofeedback equipment, we have been able to measure physical changes caused by nonphysical (mental) actions. We now know the creative aspect of the subjective dimension.

As the business manager gets in control of the subjective by practicing the countdown, visualization, and imagination exercises to be supplied in forthcoming chapters, and then by using them in the ways set forth in these pages, then, and only then can he realize and accept that he can use the subjective dimension to correct objective problems.

Human intelligence has the ability to become attuned to either the subjective or objective dimension. A business manager's problems can be approached through either objective or subjective methods.

The purpose of the Silva Method is *not* to replace objective approaches with subjective approaches. Rather, it is to *add* subjective approaches to the conventional objective approaches.

The business manager who uses only objective approaches is using only half his brain. He is, in effect, working with one hand tied behind his back. As he activates the other half of his brain, the two halves work in concert, cooperating just as two hands cooperate, to get the job done better and faster.

METHODOLOGIES FOR APPLYING SUBJECTIVE SKILLS

Just as the hands need practice in working together to accomplish a particular result, so do the two halves of the brain—the objective left and subjective right.

See that assembly worker over there? She is storing the parts in a precise way, holding the hand tool just so, and working in a sequential manner. This has been learned through practice and trial and error.

Subjective skills also need to be learned and applied. This also takes practice and methodology. Just as the assembly worker inherited the methodology through the trial and error of her supervisors and predecessors on the job, you are being provided with methodologies for applying subjective skills. These have been worked out in decades of research and application and come to you as the Silva Method.

Let us list the fundamental methodologies for utilizing subjective skills that have already been described or will be:

1. Going to level on awakening and visualizing yourself as you wish to be.

2. Going to level on awakening and giving yourself positive statements.

3. Using mental pictures to enhance memory.

4. Programming the Three Fingers Technique and using it to trigger deeper levels of awareness.

5. Making a tape and using it at level to reinforce positive programming.

6. Using the 3-to-1, 10-to-1 method and an imaginary consultant to program to awake at the best time for important programming. On awakening again, go to level with the 3-to-1, 10-to-1 method and with the expert consultant present, see three scenes. In the first, directly in front of you, the important meeting begins. In the second, slightly to the left, you make your case. In the third, slightly more to the left, there is a successful conclusion. Repeat this prior to the meeting.

7. Programming to repeat good discipline or production conditions of the past by going to level and visualizing to the right and then straight ahead.

8. Using subjective communication at level to reach a difficult person, proceeding as in (6), but with or without a consultant.

9. Using subjective communication as in (8), but adding a word or phrase to trigger compliance at the objective level.

10. Using the elimination method in connection with (6) in order to save time in making multiple decisions.

11. Using special purpose tapes, as for a time-efficient day.

12. Using the two-minute stress reliever.

13. Programming at night, as in (6), to do a job effectively (such as scheduling), including the Three Fingers Technique; then programming the next night to follow that procedure or scheduling.

14. Using calendars in visualization to program reaching goals by desired dates, moving mental pictures slightly to the left for each future goal.

15. Any suitable combinations of the above.

In the chapters ahead there will be these methodologies and more. We will begin with simple ways to go to the Alpha level and use it. Then, the emphasis will shift to applying the above and additional methodologies to more and more aspects of business management, for better and better business success.

THE COMMON GOOD

The subjective dimension is a creative—as opposed to destructive—dimension. It can be used by the clairvoyant executive to move away from problem situations in the direction of solution situations. By solution situations we mean in the direction that will benefit everybody—the most beneficial, constructive, and creative direction.

Be aware that the subjective dimension cannot be used for personal gain at the expense of somebody else. This is not a Silva Method rule. It is a fact of life.

We are accustomed to the objective dimension being used for personal gain at the expense of others. We see it every day. We see the material world being used constructively as well as destructively. We participate in both ways daily, so we tend to assume that the same is true of the subjective dimension.

The reason it is not true is that the objective dimension is one of polarity (positive and negative, good and evil, creation and destruction), but the subjective dimension, being the original dimension, is only positive, good, and creative.

Objective means that one seldom considers the benefit of the planet. Subjective means that one frequently considers the benefit of the company, the work force, the staff, the family, even the neighborhood, the nation, and the planet.

In the Silva Method, when we use the subjective dimension to change or alter a problem situation, we call it programming. This programming is always in a direction that is beneficial for everybody concerned. It has to be so, if it is to work.

BEATING THE "BLAHS"

You can use the subjective dimension to help yourself in many ways. You can improve your energy, your attitude, your health. You can even do the same for others.

Managers experience a variety of complaints that seem to

be inherent in the job, a sort of vocational hazard. Frequently, these are vague complaints, not worth mentioning to the family physician, but nevertheless real enough to interfere, to some degree, with the day's work.

Take that early morning feeling. It could be a lethargic feeling. It could be a bad taste in your mouth. It could be a disinclination to face the papers on your desk. It could be the lack of desire to speak to anybody. It could be any number of similar blocks to rolling up your sleeves and pitching in. It might be called the morning "blahs."

Shirley L. had them. She was the manager of a women's specialty store, and she felt like crawling in an inventory cabinet each morning. Instead, she drank cup after cup of coffee. That helped, but it made her short-tempered with her sales people the rest of the day.

James S. had them. It took him an hour of sitting at his desk and "waking up" before he could start processing work orders in his printing company.

Here is how they both got rid of the morning "blahs" once and for all, with the Silva Method.

The first step was to recognize that they were putting up with this morning state and to decide that they were no longer willing to let it interfere with their day.

The second step was to preprogram for a methodology that would work for them.

The third step was to use that methodology on arriving at work in the morning.

Since the first and third steps are or will be self-explanatory, I will explain the second step, what is meant by preprogramming.

PREPROGRAMMING FOR FUTURE NEEDS

Simple steps will create a change. But for those steps to succeed in creating that change, you must first program at level that this will be so. This is called preprogramming.

Once Shirley L. and James S. preprogrammed, this is what they did each morning: they put their Three Fingers together, smiled, and tapped their thymus gland for a minute or so.

Now, if you were to do this tomorrow morning, you might gain in energy and enthusiasm to a degree. But with Shirley and James, there was no "might" about it, and the degree was substantial.

You would gain to a degree because you would activate your energy by tapping your thymus gland whether you preprogrammed that or not. This is a direct physical (objective) cause-effect relationship.

You would gain to a greater degree if you had already preprogrammed the Three Fingers Technique and had been using it to cause your mind to function at a deeper level of awareness. This would work against the "blahs."

But you would gain completely if you preprogrammed that when you put a slight smile on your face, placed your three fingers together, and tapped your thymus gland for a few moments, you would instantly elevate your mood, energy, and enthusiasm.

Preprogramming means going to your level at the best time at night and stating or visualizing the actions having the desired effect.

Whenever you have future needs, you can preprogram that when you do such-and-such, those needs will be met. In this case, such-and-such is putting a smile on your face, placing your three fingers together, and tapping your thymus gland.

A word about the thymus gland. It is located in the chest about an inch and a half below the top edge of the breast plate, where the breast plate meets the throat. If you thump on the breast plate with your fingers, you vibrate the thymus gland just behind it, activating it.

Until recently, the function of the thymus has been largely unknown, but now it is suspected as having a governing purpose. It appears to regulate other systems, glands, and organs. Tapping it seems to restore normality in a number of functional situations, including abnormally low energy.

PREPROGRAMMING FOR MORNING ENERGY

Here is the procedure for preprogramming so that by smiling and tapping the thymus with your three fingers you will beat the "blahs." It presumes you have practiced going to your level according to instructions that begin in the next chapter.

1. Go to your level (3-to-1, 10-to-1) at night before falling asleep, and program yourself to wake up automatically at the best time to program yourself for this problem situation (morning "blahs").

2. When you awake during the night, again go to your level and mentally affirm, "If ever I feel low in spirits, or dull, or in the doldrums, or listless, all I need to do is put a smile on my face, place my three fingers together of either hand, and tap my thymus gland for a few moments. My spirits, energy, and enthusiasm will then be high."

3. Fall asleep from level.

The very next morning you can use this procedure to help yourself. In the privacy of your office or the washroom put a gentle smile on your face, place your three fingers together and thump your thymus vigorously for about a minute. Again, the thymus is behind the breast plate, just below the throat. You will put an immediate end to the "blahs." Your energy will increase and you will feel more ambitious and enthusiastic. Your "batteries" will be recharged.

INCREASING ENERGY FOR OTHERS

Tapping the thymus gland while putting a smile on your face is a physical procedure. The smile of enthusiasm cannot co-exist with the frown of the doldrums, so by keeping one, you dispel the other. The vibrating of the thymus gland is a physical means of stimulating body energy.

In the Silva Method such physical procedures are put to work where possible, but since the mind runs the body, mental procedures are available and are also utilized. When mental procedures are utilized, the scope of physical improvements possible is vastly increased.

There is hardly an ailment that we do not invite by our mental state. So there is hardly an ailment that will not respond positively through a positive change in that mental state.

When you walk around with the morning doldrums, you "infect" others. When you walk around with vim and enthusiasm, you excite others.

This fact alone demonstrates that your mind's field of influence extends beyond your own body. But there is also laboratory proof.

THE INFLUENCE OF CONSCIOUSNESS

In its May 1982 issue, *Science Digest* reported on how faith healers, tested in the laboratory, were able to make significant changes in one group of injured animals, compared to control groups injured in like manner. Skeptical scientists who went through the same "laying on of hands" motions as the healers caused reverse effects.

Our Silva Mind Control organization, headquartered in Laredo, Texas, has sponsored or participated in a number of research projects involving plants and animals with incontrovertible results. The mind's influence extends beyond the body. It can affect plants, animals, people, and, through them, circumstances.

Science Digest also reported that Olga Worrell, a famous faith healer, was tested for her ability to affect human physiology at a distance. Dr. Elmer Green, a biopsychologist at the Menninger Foundation, Topeka, Kansas, and Dr. C. Norman Shealy, a neurosurgeon who is past president of the American Holistic Medical Association and who heads the Pain and Health Rehabilitation Center in LaCrosse, Wisconsin, conducted the project.

Twelve volunteers, patients of Dr. Shealy who suffered from chronic pain, were hooked up one at a time to physiological monitors. Seventy feet away, Olga Worrell concentrated on each of the patients in turn. Only the research team knew when Olga began her concentration. Within seconds, there was a marked response in the monitoring equipment in four of the twelve cases. There were complex responses that included changes in the patients' brain waves, temperature, electrical quality of the skin, and respiratory and heart rates. Although this was not intended as a healing experiment, two of the patients experienced extended pain relief.

One of the most unusual patents ever granted by the United States Patent Office* was for an instrument for the "detection of emanations from materials and measurement of volumes thereof." Although its founder, radio pioneer Thomas Galen Hieronymus of Kansas City, stated in the patent that "radiations from each of the known elements of matter produce some form of energy, probably electrons," he used a prism in addition to such electronic units as a radio frequency amplifier, noninductive resistance, and variable condensers. A prism is not an electronic device. He explained, "The radiations may be refracted, focused, diffracted or otherwise manipulated in the same manner as the radiations of the visible spectrum," suggesting that this energy was not really electrical in nature.

Today, The International Association for Psychotronic Research would call this psychotronic energy. The Institute for Noetic Science would term it noetics. Other names would be given it by other cultures and groups, indicating a relationship to consciousness of the Hieronymus machine.

John Campbell, a scientist and editor of *Analog* magazine, found that the Hieronymus machine worked: Seeds were planted in a dark basement. Wires led to some of the young shoots from outside sunlit plates through the machine. These plants turned green and grew in the dark. Others that were not so connected did not.

When Campbell published his findings, Arthur M. Young, president of the Foundation for the Study of Consciousness, suggested to Campbell that it was really the human mind at work. Campbell then used only a paper diagram of the circuits and it worked just as well!

OTHERS RESONATE WITH YOU

If you are in the doldrums, you are affecting others with whom you work. It makes no difference if you are hiding in

---

*No. 2, 482, 773 granted in 1949.

your office. The energy of consciousness, by any name, penetrates walls and crosses distances.

If you are enthusiastic and vibrant, you are also affecting others with whom you work. Yes, they are affected by hearing you and seeing you, but even without the benefit of these senses, their own spirits are lifted by yours. You are a "manager" in more ways than you have perhaps realized.

So, it is important to the business manager to be able to use the Alpha level to correct his own deficiency in attitude, energy, or health, not for just personal reasons but for the benefit of his personnel and his company.

The more others respect your position and the more rapport you have with them, the more they respond positively to you.

You have a responsibility to keep yourself in top physical and mental shape more than does a less influential person. The Alpha level is your control. At ten cycles per second, your brain waves are at a normalizing harmony.

ENDING A HEADACHE

Suppose you are the victim of an occasional tension headache, and you have practiced the procedures that enable you to go to the Alpha level. (Instructions to go to Alpha level begin in Chapter 5.) How can you use the Alpha level to end such a pesky condition?

1. Close your eyes. Turn them slightly upwards. Count backwards from 5 to 1.

2. Remain with your eyes closed at the Alpha level for about three to five minutes.

3. During these few minutes you can be thinking about what needs to be done in any project on which you are working, analyzing situations, taking inventory of the past.

4. Even if some remnants of the discomfort still exist at the end of three to five minutes, count yourself up, reminding yourself that when you reach the count of 5, you will be wide awake, and feeling better than before.

Minutes spent at Alpha are not minutes wasted. Minutes spent at Alpha can be the most valuable minutes of the day.

The practiced person can go to Alpha with eyes open if necessary. By looking slightly upwards and unfocusing the eyes, Alpha brain frequencies are triggered. It feels like daydreaming. This daydreaming state has been stigmatized by our society as a waste of time. It is exactly the opposite. It is one of the most creative uses we can make of time.

Being at Alpha automatically disconnects the cause of the headache, which is Beta-related. But why not make use of this being at Alpha for even more benefit than ending a headache? That is why I suggest you let your mind think about your work during these few Alpha minutes. Such thinking should be permitted to come naturally in a day-dreaming way.

"It did not work," said Tom B. to one of our Silva Method lecturers.

"Tell me what you did," replied the lecturer.

"I relaxed comfortably, closed my eyes, turned them upwards, and counted from 5 to 1. Then I thought about the problem I was involved in. After about three or four minutes, I counted myself up 1 to 5, asserting that I would be feeling wide awake and better. But I felt just as bad. I still had the headache."

"What is the problem?" asked the lecturer.

"The computer programmer. I tell him how to proceed. He is supposed to do it. But the personnel department wants to save money, so it hires 'greenhorns.' I wind up having to do it myself, and I just don't have the time."

Can you advise Tom B.? Of course you can:

"Tom, next time don't think about that problem. That is what is giving you the headache. Instead, while at Alpha, let your mind roam on a broader scale. Think about the day, not the minute. Think about the progress of the week or the month, rather than about the current tension."

With that change, Tom was able to control his headaches.

When we worry at the Alpha level, we move up to Beta. To stay at Alpha we need to have more peaceful, worry-free thoughts.

FALLING ASLEEP

Alpha is packed with benefits. To the clairvoyant executive who has been practicing and using the Alpha level related to the methodologies and applications provided herein, the Alpha level is a source of relief, a source of energy, a source of solutions, and a source of ideas. It provides relief from the "blahs," relief from headaches, relief from what else? The list is endless. As many discomforts and abnormalities as man can think of, he can also obtain relief from at the Alpha level.

Tens of millions of people suffer from insomnia. They begin by lying awake for hours worrying whether they will be able to get a good night's sleep. Worrying is Beta. To reach sleep, you need to pass through Alpha.

Over $200 million a year is spent on prescription sleeping pills. In 1976, doctors at the Sleep Disorder Clinic at Stanford University reported that about forty percent of insomnia patients were losing sleep because they had become dependent on the very drugs they were taking for their insomnia. When these patients were gradually withdrawn from the drugs, they slept an average of twenty percent more and many had no more sleep problems.

The business executive who lies awake worrying is better off lying awake worrying than he is taking sleeping pills. Many of these can be harmful and can lead to escalating dosages, drug intolerance, and drug-induced insomnia. The clairvoyant business executive who has acquired the ability to function at Alpha has a far better solution available to him for insomnia than pills.

The Alpha level is halfway to sleep. Deep sleep is Delta, under four cycles per second. To go from an awake Beta state, twenty cycles, to an asleep state you have to pass through Alpha, ten cycles. Once you know how to go to Alpha, why not go there when you want to fall asleep? It's a shorter trip.

1. If you desire to fall asleep, close your eyes and turn them slightly upward.

2. Count backwards from 5 to 1—once you have practiced this as described later.

3. Begin to count sheep backwards, starting from 100.

It is unlikely that you will reach the count of 50, much less the count of 1. It is boring watching look-alike sheep jumping over a fence. The procedure you will learn, starting in Chapter 5, involves counting backwards from 100 to 1. This is boring, too, but a necessary first step in the process of relaxation. You use it to relax to the Alpha level. You can use it to go even deeper—to sleep.

What will make this work even better for you? Pre-programming it. Do this some night in the manner described earlier in this chapter. Program yourself to awaken during the night; when you do, go to level and program that when you are not falling asleep all you have to do is to go to level and count sheep backwards. "Each count brings me closer to healthful sleep." And this will be so.

A business manager needs his sleep. A clairvoyant business manager, in control of his mind, gets that sleep.

THE MIND CAN DO ANYTHING, IF . . .

The mind can indeed do anything; but for most of us, it doesn't. The reason is that we don't believe it can.

As you come to understand what your mind can do, you can do more. Your desire then becomes powered by your expectation and belief. Your mental "foot" is off the brake and on the accelerator.

A good place to start is with the physical and emotional obstacles to full managerial performance. We have covered the morning "blahs," headaches, and lack of sleep. There are scores of other pesky feelings, attitudes and symptoms that "won't go away."

I have good news. They will go away. They are like invited guests. End the atmosphere of hospitality and the guests leave. Desire, expectancy, and belief in the unwanted guests' leaving changes that atmosphere. Programming opens the door and slams it behind them.

THE METHODOLOGY AS A FLEXIBLE TOOL

Your hands can do anything, when you use them, and with the right tools. Your mind can do anything, when you use it, and with the right tools. Your main tool to combat unwanted attitudes, emotions, personality quirks, listlessness and boredom is the Alpha level.

Other tools at your disposal are visualization, imagination, affirmation, imaginary consultants, triggering techniques. More will be provided as we progress, but these are all you need to translate desire, expectation, and belief into the ending of unwanted states and the beginning of refreshing new states.

Which tool do you use to translate:

Boredom into enthusiasm?
A laissez-faire attitude into ambition?
Detachment into involvement?
"The miseries" into wellbeing?
Giving up into digging in?

Here the analogy of a tool begins to break down. A screwdriver cannot be used to hammer a nail, or a hammer to turn a screw.

Visualization can be used as a tool in all of the above cases. So can imagination. So can the Three Fingers Technique, and other triggering devices.

It might be better to use the analogy of first aid, second aid, and permanent aid. You can use your mind to help yourself out of boredom temporarily on the spot—the "band-aid" treatment; or you can preprogram and reinforce for more permanent results.

Let us list three approaches in the order of permanence:

1. Go to level on the spot. State the problem. ("I am bored.") State your desire for a change. ("I don't want to be bored; I want to be enthusiastic.") Program for that change. ("When I count to five and open my eyes I will

no longer be bored, I will restore my natural enthusiasm.") Count to five and reaffirm as you open your eyes. ("I am enthusiastic.")

2. When you awake in the morning, go to level. Visualize yourself at work. See yourself as you wish to be.

3. When you go to bed at night, program to awake at the best time. When you awake, go to level and visualize yourself as you are. Move the picture to the left and see yourself using a triggering technique to change (putting a smile on your face, or putting your three fingers together, or taking a deep breath, etc.). Move the picture more to the left and see yourself as you wish to be. Fall asleep from level. Reinforce by repeating this procedure for several nights or some night in the future. During the day, whenever you feel the unwanted condition, use the triggering technique to make an instant change.

BURNOUT

Boredom, a laissez-faire attitude, detachment, the miseries, giving up, and a score of other lackadaisical aspects all add up to the nemesis of every business manager—burnout. Managers who use the Silva Method are not candidates for burnout.

Recently, twenty-five members of the management staff of RCA Records Division in New Jersey went through the Silva Method training in a controlled project. An evaluation was made of each manager before and after the training. The instrument of evaluation chosen was Cattell's 16 PF Personality Test.

The test was administered to all twenty-five individuals on Monday morning prior to the start of the training, under the supervision of George T. DeSau, Ed.D., one of our valued consultants and lecturers. The training was given Monday through Thursday by Eileen Buehler, certified Silva Method lecturer. Twenty persons completed the training and took the posttesting.

Three quarters of those tested again showed significant changes for the better. The others showed little or no change. The greatest change for the better was in their ability to "adjust to the facts; directing emotional energies along integrated as opposed to impulse channels; and being calmer and more emotionally mature."

The second greatest change for the better was in becoming more "assertive, competitive, and able to find enjoyment in meeting challenges."

The third greatest change was in the participants perceiving themselves as more relaxed and composed; a vital improvement considering that, aside from its emotionally and physically depleting effects, excessive stress is recognized as a deterrent to effective decision making.

In addition, the group showed significant improvement in skills reflective of self and organizational management. It was an impressive demonstration of the Silva Method's appropriateness for that special person known as the business manager.

Certainly, the business manager who is more emotionally mature, who is more assertive, competitive and able to find enjoyment in meeting challenges, and who is more composed is hardly a candidate for burnout.

4

How You Gain in Managerial Skills When You Control Your Mind

There are over four million people who now use the Silva Method. They include top-level executives and managers in domestic and foreign companies. They have enjoyed accelerated personal and business success simply because they know how to bring more intelligence to bear on competitive situations whenever needed.

A NEW DIMENSION OF THINKING

The increment of intelligence is far from minuscule. It is an impressive leap. Smart managers have become ingenious managers. The key word to describe this added dimension in thinking is "clairvoyance." It is the ability to be able to see things more clearly.

The Silva Method of mental training helps people to become clairvoyants. As used in this book, a clairvoyant is a person with acute intuitive insight or perception, who is able to perceive ideas, facts, or events outside of the ordinary range of human senses.

A clairvoyant uses two dimensions of thinking, two sets of senses, and both brain hemispheres—the left hemisphere that deals with objective things, and the right one that deals with subjective things.

A person who is not clairvoyant uses only one dimension of thinking, one set of senses, and only the left brain hemisphere to think with. His is an objective world. He has no conscious access to the vast information and intelligence available through the subconscious.

When a person learns how to think with the right hemisphere, the part of our brain largely ignored by modern education, it is like using the subconscious consciously. It adds a new dimension to thinking.

Executives at Hoffmann-LaRoche, a leading pharmaceutical firm, have been trained in the Silva Method and are using this new dimension of thinking. The firm has since taken some bold new steps that have proven profitable.

Mary Kay Cosmetics, a leading skin care product company, has embarked on a program of having personnel trained in the Silva Method, because of the initial sales effectiveness.

Recently, twenty-five managers at RCA Records Division in New Jersey went through the Silva Method training in a controlled project. The emphatic results were detailed in the previous chapter.

Officially and unofficially, firms in the United States as well as Canada, Mexico, Central, and South America now have added a new dimension of thinking using the Silva Method, with interest spreading to Europe, Australia, and parts of Asia.

This new level of thinking requires no special skill or IQ. It requires no effort, no concentration, no long years of training. It is available to anybody, regardless of age, race, creed, sex, or level of education. It is as easy as closing your eyes and picturing a dollar bill.

THE MIND OUT OF CONTROL

It has been said that the mind is like a drunken monkey, wandering here and there and occasionally stumbling on solutions. Although this gives an uncomplimentary picture of supposedly intelligent man, it is true that man is mentally getting in his own way. He is using only a fraction of his intelligence.

There is a way to activate more of your mind to go to work for you. In India, they have a way, but that way takes years of training for only the first step—to stop the monkey from wandering.

There is another way. It takes less than two months. It is revealed in this book. It leads you along the path of actualizing your potential for being a genius. It is called the Silva Method of controlling your mind.

A plant manager is faced with a situation in which the productivity of a key worker has plummeted. He invites the man into his office for a talk. The man denies any family problem, emotional problem, or health problem. The plant manager waits until the man has left his office. He then closes his eyes, takes a few deep breaths and sits quietly while he visualizes the man. In a few minutes, he opens his eyes. He calls the man in for another talk. He identifies a family problem the man is having. The man reluctantly confirms his "guess." The manager recommends a counselor. The problem is solved. The man's high productivity is resumed.

THE MIND UNDER CONTROL

What happened during those few moments that the plant manager sat with his eyes closed? He used his mind in a way that is not taught to us in school or college. It is a natural use of the mind. It is the mind under control.

The mind under control is helping managers to solve inventory problems, find lost records, increase safety, improve plant efficiency, and win support for creative proposals.

The mind under your control can be ten times more intelligent than the drunken monkey.

Had we put the electrodes of a brain electroencephalograph (EEG) on this manager's head when he closed his eyes, we would have seen his brain waves slow down gradually from twenty cycles per second to ten cycles per second. The manager, by going through a simple mental process, was slowing his brain waves so that he could then perform at a different level of mind. It is called the Alpha level.

THE EMERGING ALPHA

You will not find Alpha mind approaches to learning in school textbooks, methodologies, or curricula. Yet, you may hear about how employees at the Weyerhaeuser Company in Tacoma, Washington have been meeting in small groups since 1972 for experimental right brain learning—using mental imagery to enhance problem-solving abilities. This is done at the Alpha level, albeit with an approach different from the Silva Method.

You may hear about such terms as "Super Learning," "Optimalearning," and "Suggestology"—all commercial approaches to teaching participants how to use relaxation, Alpha, to evoke their best performances on any task. You may hear about stress management more frequently as a key to better performance levels, again, using the Alpha level.

Our educational system has a built-in stabilizer. It is difficult, if not impossible, to rock the boat.

As research reveals the awesome potential of the human mind and new ways to activate it, schools drift placidly on teaching the same rigid subjects and in dehumanizing ways. It may be many years before schools respond to changing values in society and to new scientific findings relating to the mind. Meanwhile, we all need to do our part as teachers, parents, or students in encouraging such progress.

Certainly, we need to do our part as managers in the business world to minimize disharmony, waste, inefficiency, doldrums, indecision, and inaccuracy and, through using more of our mind to work for us, maximize teamwork, motivation, enthusiasm, creativity, ingenuity, productivity and profits.

INTELLIGENCE SABOTAGED

When we think logically to come to a decision, we are using the brain's left hemisphere. When we permit our gut feeling to lead us to a decision, we are using the brain's right hemisphere.

If we were to habitually do one but not the other, we would be, in effect, doing our job with one arm tied behind our back. If we were to habitually use our logical thinking alone, we would be doing our job with our right arm tied behind our back.

Because our education, in school, college and on the job, is largely left brain, we are sabotaging our own intelligence. It is as if we are doing our job in a half-brained manner, one-half of our brain sitting on the sidelines.

I mentioned a few new approaches to learning that utilize more of the right brain. They are to be applauded; but they emphasize only learning a new language or only memorizing more easily. Take another recent approach, Synetics. It accelerates learning by the use of metaphors. Students are encouraged to "feel" a problem or a situation. This is a commendable step forward. The more schools that adopt this, the better.

But what about the rest of us who are out of school, who do not want to learn another language, or memorize easier? How do we activate the right brain to go to work for us? How do we get out of the half-brain habit? How do we stop sabotaging our own intelligence?

CONTROLLING YOUR MIND AT ALPHA

Business managers are on the firing line. The pressures, the catch-22's, the competition, the internal politics, the deadlines and the conflicts make business managers prime candidates for loneliness, fear of failure, anxiety and stress.

Business managers who learn the Silva Method of Mind Control, as presented on the pages ahead, are able to "push their own buttons." They move from being creatures of circumstance to creators of circumstance. Not only do they use the Alpha level of mind to insulate themselves from stressful factors, they use it to program themselves to ride formerly threatening waves to new peaks of personal and business success.

THE POSSIBLE MANAGER

Inside every business manager is an ultimate, or possible, business manager trying to get out. We all have the potential for brilliance; not all of us realize that potential.

We are like computers. We have programmed ourselves to go thus far and no further. We have developed a set of limitations over the years, based on what our parents, teachers, bankers, peers, and supervisors have taught us. Within that framework of limitations we conduct our business and social life. We have self-images. We live our lives within the confines of the concept we have of ourselves. It is a prison of our own making.

One day, we try the door. We find that it was never locked, and the possible human in us is able to emerge. The Silva Method is such a door. Using it, the business manager is able to:

– Improve self-confidence and self-esteem.

– Eliminate health-sapping habits.

– End nervousness, tension headaches, and other pesky health problems.

– Enhance relationships with personnel.

– Enlist support from superiors.

– Inspire discipline and efficiency.

– Get restful sleep nightly without drugs.

– Maintain a positive mental attitude.

– Manage time so as to get more done.

– Plan personal and business goals and achieve them.

– Ride unperturbedly through stress.

– Develop a super memory.

– Trigger more mental capacity when needed.

– Be a dynamo of energy and enthusiasm.

– Tap a source spring of creative ideas.

– Stand as an inspiration to others.

– Make this a better world to live in.

FROM SUCCESS TO FAILURE

Man loses job. Man becomes depressed. Man is overwhelmed by a sense of failure. Man separates himself from relatives and friends. Depression deepens. Interviews fail. Man claims, "I'm a loser." Sound familiar?

It happens every day—but not when you learn the Silva Method. And it need never happen to you once you train yourself according to the procedures in this book. The Silva Method puts you in charge of your mind. You understand all the positive aspects of yourself. As you begin to "push the positive buttons," you begin identifying with success. You transfer positive energy, or feeling, to others. You light up in their eyes as a winner.

B.A., twenty-four, of Florida, got a job in the space program at Cape Kennedy. He was proudly realizing the dream of his youth. But, within a year, he was out. It was a blow. He had not saved any money. His feeling of pride turned to a feeling of inferiority. He heard about the Silva Method. He had to borrow the tuition money from a friend.

He began using what he learned immediately to program himself to find a job. Within one week he was working. It was not an ideal job, but it enabled him to save money during his first year with that company. He enjoyed making waterbeds. He used the money to buy waterbed materials. Now he used his Silva Method training to "see" himself in the waterbed business. He went to his Alpha level of mind for two or three minutes every day and "saw" himself conducting a waterbed business successfully.

First, he manufactured the beds at night in his home and sold them on weekends. Soon he had to rent a vacant store. He still worked weekdays at his job, programmed daily, and made profitable sales on Saturdays and Sundays. Within one more year he had two full-time stores and was well on his way to grossing a million dollars a year.

B.A.'s story is not sensational, but it is typical of everyday uses to which the Silva Method is being put by countless business people. These business people do not fill unemployment offices, bankruptcy courts, or hospitals; they fill bank accounts.

If our friend B.A. is the microcosm, here is the macrocosm.

FROM NIGHT INTO DAY

The NDM Corporation, located on the Miami River in Dayton, Ohio, manufactures machines used in the medical field and also develops plastics for use within the human body. Its president took the Silva Method training course, and decided to have all 550 employees trained.

The training course started with eighty employees at a time, most of whom were at management levels. In one of the first classes was a chemist working to find a new plastic that the body would not reject and that could be used for arteries in bypass surgery. This chemist decided to use a Silva Method technique that puts the mind to work on a problem while you are asleep.

He awoke during the night with a vivid recollection of a dream about a formula. He wrote it down. When he examined the formula at the plant in the morning, it was almost identical to one he had already tried with negative results. "Why waste time," a colleague said, "we have already worked on that one." But he had a gut feeling that the small difference in the formula might make a big difference. Over the objections of his colleague, he put together a sample, tested it, and it worked!

When we dream, the mind comes up from deep levels of sleep to the Alpha level. At the Alpha level, the mind is capable of obtaining solutions in genius-like ways. Answers are brought from the darkness of the unconscious to the light of day.

COMPUTER WITH THIRTY BILLION COMPONENTS

The brain weighs about three pounds. It contains about thirty billion neurons. These act as centers of brain activity pretty much the same way as do components of a computer.

Brain neurons are connected to each other through an elaborate network. Altogether, some 100 trillion trillion atoms "cooperate" in our brain's neurons and connectors.

We would all benefit if we understood that our limits are not dictated by our pay envelope, or our personnel folder, or our education, but that these 100 trillion trillion atoms are a more accurate gauge of those limits.

But what does 100 trillion trillion mean? To comprehend that number better and therefore to understand your personal limitations better, it might be helpful to pretend for a moment that an atom is the size of a tiny air gun pellet. If you are sitting right now in an average-size living room, and if you were to fill the room from floor to ceiling, wall to wall with air gun pellets, would you have enough? Yes, you would and then some.

Hold this book with one hand and snap the fingers of your other hand every second. Imagine you are filling such a room, floor to ceiling every second with air gun pellets—with every snap of the fingers another room is filled. Then stop when you feel you may have used up the 100 trillion trillion air gun pellets.

Have you stopped yet? You should not have. The truth is that it would take forty million years before you would run out of pellets!

The brain is a phenomenal computer. The portion of our brain that we use in social, business, and professional life is impressive enough, but that is only about one-tenth of its true capacity.

OFFICE OF THE FUTURE

A recent survey revealed that offices in the United States handle approximately 325 billion documents a year, with the volume growing by over 70 billion pieces a year. This blizzard of paper has been paralyzing the business office. Electronic filing promises relief. As you know, the electronic "filing cabinets" are computer tapes, video disks, and microform products. Magazines often describe and picture the executive work station of tomorrow. They depict the executive facing a single large video screen flashing the day's mail and interoffice memos. The screen also serves as a graphics panel, a video monitor, and a word-processing display. A voice—the executive's—directs all of these functions. Now, add one more extraordinary feature—you, the clairvoyant executive—in *your* office of tomorrow.

- You are able to handle difficult people without speaking a single word to them.

- You are able to assist a heavy drinker to break his habit without his knowing of your help.

- You are able to get more work done each day and to help others to do the same with no sweat or stress.

- You are able to trigger creative ideas that stop the competition dead in their tracks.

- You are able to write better reports and to grasp and retain what you read in others' reports.

- You are able to trust your gut feelings even when they are contrary to others' opinions, and make sound intuitive decisions.

- You are able to solve sudden problems and long-range problems in ways that may surprise you.

- You are able to say the right thing at meetings, and thus contribute to the sought-after goal.

- You are able to avoid burnout, to control your own energy, enthusiasm, and good health.

- You are able to positively affect your own progress and your company's profits.

THE MANAGER OF THE FUTURE—TODAY

The manager of the future knows how to activate the thirty billion components of his or her cranial computer to solve problems, retrieve information, and communicate directly with other cranial computers, effortlessly and quickly.

The future manager's "on" switch is the Alpha level. His video monitor is his "mental screen." He can detect problems at a distance without being there, and he can make corrections, also at a distance.

When you complete the Silva Method training on these pages, you become the manager of the future today.

The right half of your cranial computer can transcend space in this manner, and time as well. You can turn the clock back to find causes. You can turn the clock ahead to foresee effects.

You can also be more of a human being in:

– Dealing with spouse, in-laws, family

– Handling personnel matters

– Facing a supervisor or subordinate

– Meeting deadlines

– Giving speeches or oral reports

– Making compassionate decisions

– Closing a sale

– Enlisting friends and supporters

Unlike the office of tomorrow which is only partly available today, the business manager of the future has arrived. His time has come. It has come largely as a result of the Silva Method for using more of the mind.

MAGIC IN BUSINESS?

Recently, the business pages carried an item about a novelty item that was enjoying phenomenal sales—a magic wand. Fourteen inches long, the wand is a clear acrylic rod with an acrylic sphere and star enclosed at the top. Mrs. Laura Chatain began selling the wands from an abandoned laundromat in Harbor Springs, Michigan. With only $1,500 of promotional expense, she soon reached a volume of 500 of the $5 wands shipped daily. At the time of the news item she had shipped over 100,000 wands.

Queried on how or why the wand works to get a raise, pursue a romance, or quit smoking, Mrs. Chatain quoted psychologists who attributed its success to imagery and visualization. I agree with that. But it is only part of the story. I would like to offer two more factors—expectation and belief.

Expectation and belief comprise the "magic" of success in business and in life. Without them, little is possible. With them, just about anything is possible.

We now know enough about the human brain to understand how expectation and belief make innocuous sugar pills, thought by the patient to be powerful prescribed medicine, work magical cures. We now know enough about the human brain to understand how expectation and belief are the critical factors that determine whether a desired goal is reached or not. We now know enough about the human brain to understand how lack of expectation and belief is equivalent to a programming for failure and how the existence of expectation and belief is equivalent to a programming for success.

We understand expectation and belief scientifically, but the fact remains: they work "like magic."

Ed B., a business manager in Albuquerque, New Mexico, programmed that whenever he put his three fingers together, he would say the right thing in negotiations with suppliers and they would accept his offers more readily. It worked. It is a Silva Method technique you will learn in the pages ahead.

Neva D. of Dallas, Texas, manager of an industrial scales business, programmed that potential customers would be more receptive to her sales talk. Her sales volume rose. She used a Silva Method technique you will learn in the pages ahead.

James N. of San Antonio, Texas, manager of a real estate investment firm, programmed to be the first to be appointed by people who decide to sell property. He was—time and time again. He, too, used a Silva Method technique which he now teaches in the Silva Method training and which you will learn in the pages ahead.

All three had something in common, a common denominator, if you will—desire, expectation and belief.

THE POWER OF DESIRE, EXPECTATION, AND BELIEF

Desire, expectation, and belief are words that express feelings. Feelings are subjective; they cannot be photographed or measured. Therefore, they are not real. Right?

Wrong! Desire has led to the creation of all that has been made by man on this planet. Expectation and belief have energized that desire.

It is as if a real energy were at work; and it might very well be. Hundreds of scientists in every discipline have been meeting every two years for the past eight years, under the sponsorship of the Association For Psychotronic Research to share their research on the "energy of consciousness." Also, Edgar Mitchell, United States astronaut, formed the Institute for Noetic Sciences, for similar purposes. SRI (formerly Stanford Research Institute) of Palo Alto, California, has been working with gifted individuals who become able to do real physical work with this mental energy.

Whatever name you give this energy—and there have been a flurry of names—it is the same real energy. It is focused by the mind. It is creative.

"I do not desire," "I do not expect," or "I do not believe" keeps this energy in "Off."

"I desire" turns it on. "I expect" turns up the voltage. "I believe" provides the needed power.

With the Silva Method of controlling your mind, you harness this creative energy for yourself and for your company. What you will experience I can only talk about at this point.

THE WORDS VERSUS THE EXPERIENCE

The name Hoffmann-LaRoche is famous for pharmaceuticals. In 1973, some six years after the Silva Method was launched and when there were only 100,000 graduates in the

United States, Canada, Mexico, and England, the training was sponsored for employees by Roche's employee development department. When a sampling of 150 employees had been trained, the company's newsletter ran a full page story on the project which included a number of statements from these employees. Here are some excerpts from managers and others:

— *Merchandising Director*— "It gave me a new sense of awareness about myself and the importance of interacting and working with fellow employees. I am applying what I learned by trying to develop the ability to channel my interests and accomplishments so there is less wasted time and motion."

— *Assistant Biochemist*— "I have a very favorable impression of the Mind Control course, but then I don't know of anyone who took the course who doesn't. My whole mental attitude has changed; as a result, I'm convinced that good things really happen when you look at life positively."

— *Administrator, Personnel*— "It is one of the best things that has happened to me . . . helped me develop an inner peace and build up my confidence. As for its benefits to Roche, can you imagine 2,000 employees with their minds geared to positive thinking? This company would be flying."

These are all fine testimonials. But now listen to these three key people:

— *Senior Group Chief, Chemical Production*— "The course is effective only for those willing to listen and take an active interest in the subject."

— *Senior Systems Analyst*— "The program heightens sensitivity to other people and makes us more aware of intuitive experiences that the rational mind tends to deny."

— *Plant Services Supervisor*—"The key to success is belief. You have to believe in the power of the mind in order to enjoy the course and get anything out of it."

Is not the Chief talking about *desire,* the Analyst talking about *expectation,* and the Supervisor talking about *belief?*

Others expressed the polarity of belief that existed between those who took the training and those who had not yet taken it. Said an Information Systems Specialist, "I've been laughed at by those who don't believe that the human mind can do anything more than it is doing now."

A Senior Biochemist put it this way. "There is a definite credibility gap and high level of skepticism among those who have not been exposed to the Mind Control Course."

What emerges from these statements is not what the training entails, not the Alpha experience; but the changes in desire, expectation, and belief that come as a normal outgrowth of the experience.

That experience itself is hard to put into statements. It was even harder ten years ago when these statements were made. Certainly it was hard for scientifically oriented people in those days to describe experiences that went beyond science's ability to understand or accept—especially for publication in their own company paper.

It is a different situation today.

PSI EXPERIENCES NO LONGER UNSPEAKABLE

We are in a new age. The mention of the PSI factor, ESP, psychic functioning, clairvoyance, is no longer a taboo subject. Science no longer denies these powers of the mind.

You do not have to shield this page from view. The paranormal is no longer "X-rated."

Those who learn the Silva Method find themselves at new levels of desire, expectation, and belief in the powers of their own mind to help them in business. As a result, they are able to function at a higher level, with greater perception and keener insight. They attain greater awareness, heightened efficiency, more confidence, and an inner peace.

But what is even more dramatic and valuable to those business people are the "superhuman" experiences. Here are some examples:

– While you are at a meeting, you put the first two fingers together with the thumb (either hand) and you find you are saying the right thing at the right time—you function at a deeper level of awareness.

– It is 3:00 P.M. and you have had a trying day. You close your eyes, take three deep breaths, give yourself a simple instruction, and when you open your eyes, you are wide awake, full of energy and "gung ho."

– You need fifteen or twenty items from the stockroom. Faster than you can write them down, you make mental pictures in a special way and are able to remember them easily at the order desk.

– You have a tough problem. No solution presents itself. That night before falling asleep, you program your mental computer to awaken at an appropriate time to solve that problem. When you awaken, you use a special mental procedure and the answer comes.

– You are stymied. Maybe it has to do with finding a location for a new outlet, acquiring the right person to fill a job, pursuing the right path to expand sales. You go to your relaxed state of mind and picture the problem. You are able to obtain the solution in a way that you will learn about in a future chapter; and the solution comes about.

– A machine is not functioning properly. If you knew what the problem was, you might avoid taking it out of production for a long period of overhaul time. You use the Silva Method. Your attention is called to a malfunctioning part. It is replaced and the problem is solved.

– Your advertisements or commercials are not working as well as you would like. You make one small change which you acquire through the Silva Method. It has immediate results.

– You suspect a person of pilfering tools. You use the Silva Method for subjective communication. Without your having to say a single word to the person, the pilfering stops.

– The competition has something new going for it. You do not know what it is. All you know is that they are taking customers away. You have an imaginary conversation with their president at the Alpha level. You find out what they are doing. You take countermeasures.

– A snag has developed in the creation of a new product. It could take limitless research to overcome. You go through a procedure of the Silva Method and that night you obtain information that shows you how to get around the snag. It works.

These are all specific examples of a few of the ways that business managers use the Silva Method, and that you will be able to apply using the instructions in the chapters ahead.

MANAGER APPLICATIONS

"Incredible!" "Far out!" "Real crazy!"

These are typical remarks from people who use the Silva Method describing the way they have just performed. They are comparing the power of their minds, newly activated by the Silva Method, to the old ways in which they have been using their minds.

Business managers use the Silva Method to:

– Handle the unreasonable supervisor.

– Deal with people who quarrel amongst themselves on the job.

– Boost initiative in themselves and others.

– Improve subordinates' abilities to follow instructions.

– Smooth over problems with managers of other departments.

– Eliminate feelings of unfair treatment.

– Solve community relations problems.

– Reduce discipline problems.

– Correct abuses of authority—overuse or underuse.

– Improve punctuality.

– Solve problems in design, production, marketing.

– Communicate more effectively.

– Heighten moral as well as physical and mental well-being.

– Harmonize labor-management relationships.

These are general and represent only a fragment of the whole canvas. You have glimpsed other fragments in the opening chapters. The full picture for you as a manager will be seen as you progress through this book. You will be able to particularize applications for your company, your department, your needs.

PROSPERITY STARTS IN THE SUBJECTIVE DIMENSION

With no formal education, I have been successful and prosperous all my life and in all areas of my life. There are many sides to prosperity: your health can prosper; so can your relationships with family or colleagues. We can experience a rich joy in living. We can have a storehouse of memories of problems solved and people served. We can have all the money we need.

Most people equate prosperity with material success—money. However, as important as the money is, it cannot be fully enjoyed without good health, or if you have family problems, or your work is boring.

To attain prosperity in its fullest sense, we need clairvoyance, confidence, enthusiasm, and work.

Read that sentence again. "Fullest sense" means not only the money but the health and opportunity to enjoy prosperity. And the word "clairvoyance" seems to add a strange dimension to the three standard ingredients that appear in all the classic texts.

I once appeared as a speaker on the same rostrum with W. Clement Stone, head of a major insurance organization and author of several successful "success" books. He has accumulated great wealth and teaches his employees and others his method. As I listened and watched, I could see that W. Clement Stone is a natural clairvoyant, who learned to use and trust his intuition at an early age. I am also a clairvoyant. It takes one to know one.

What is a clairvoyant? It is a person who "receives" information beyond the range of his eyes or senses, a person who intuitively "sees" decisions and solutions in a way that appears to be guesswork, but that proves to be accurate and dependable.

Who is a clairvoyant? Everybody is. You are. When your eyes are closed you cannot see. When you are closed to clairvoyance, you cannot be intuitive. The objective work-a-day world of living has a way of closing us to clairvoyance, because clairvoyance functions under our control only at the subjective level.

With the Silva Method, as explained in the pages ahead, you learn to function at the subjective level when the need arises. You learn to find and use your clairvoyance.

As you practice, you build confidence. Confidence activates expectancy and enthusiasm. Then, the work flows easily, joyfully, and prosperity is manifested.

This material world springs from energy. Destroy the atom and it returns to that energy form. Energy is cause. Material is effect. The energy of our consciousness is at this causal, creative level. When we withdraw from the objective world mentally, and go to the subjective level, we are using our mental energy in a causal, creative dimension.

If you need something in the objective world, you can set the creative wheels in motion at the subjective dimension. This is the activation of clairvoyance. This is the beginning of prosperity. This is the way of the super manager.

Welcome to the subjective dimension.

5

The Silva Method for Getting More of Your Mind to Work for You

I wish I could explain easily how you can relax and slow your brain waves to go to the subjective dimension.

I wish I could put in a nutshell all of the ways you can use the subjective dimension to benefit yourself and your work.

I wish I could explain concisely how the subjective dimension is not limited by time and space and how you can function creatively in that dimension in ways that defy objective dimension laws.

I believe that my many decades of research and experience in this field will enable me to do this.

I believe that the assistance of my writing associate, Dr. Robert B. Stone, who has had scores of self-help books published, will enable me to get this done.

I believe that the skills of the publisher's staff will assure success in this goal.

I expect that success. I expect a useful guide for managers. I expect it to be used widely by business managers and executives.

These have been my desires, beliefs, and expectations. I have gone to the subjective dimensions repeatedly to visualize the project. The normal process of creation has taken place. The book is in your hands.

I am continuing the process. I visualize you putting the book down, relaxing to go to the subjective dimension in order to experience and learn the Silva Method, and using it to make this a better world to live in.

We learn about the objective physical world in school, objectively. But we do not learn about the subjective dimension at school. The only way we can learn about it is subjectively.

In school or college, we cannot close our eyes, turn off the physical realm and go to the imaginative or subjective dimension. When we tried that in elementary school, we got our knuckles rapped; in high school, we had to do an extra assignment; in college, we got labeled.

You can now go to the imaginative, subjective dimension without fear of reprisal. Instead, go to that level with the expectation of reward.

TEN BRAIN CYCLES PER SECOND

The Silva Method of mental training helps a person to function with full awareness at a state of mind usually associated with hallucinating or being half asleep. It is a state we pass through when falling asleep at night and awakening in the morning.

About ninety percent of all people function at twenty cycles per second of brain pulsations when awake. They do their thinking and problem solving at twenty cycles. So they do both their physical working and their mental working at the same brain frequency. The other ten percent do their thinking at ten cycles per second. So they think at ten cycles and work at twenty cycles. You cannot beat working at twenty cycles. It is the optimum level for physical work. But you can beat thinking at twenty cycles. The optimum level for thinking is about ten cycles.

At about ten cycles, the right hemisphere more fully joins in the thinking process. Intuition is activated. Clairvoyance is turned on. These cycles are energy pulsations that are measurable with brain electroencephalograph equipment. The dominant frequency is called Beta, Alpha, Theta or Delta, going from rapid when under stress to slower when relaxed, to slower still when asleep.

We will call 10 cycles Alpha. Actually it is defined more broadly:

Beta	14-21 or over
Alpha	7-14
Theta	4-7
Delta	½-4

The middle of Alpha is 10½. If you divide the usual maximum brain wave pulsation rate (21) by 2, you also get 10½. For our purposes, we will simplify the matter by using the word Alpha and 10 cycles interchangeably.

We accept the ten-cycle brain frequency to be the center of human intelligence. It is the crossover point where both brain hemispheres—right and left—function according to the need of the moment. It is the optimum frequency at which to educate human intelligence in the use of all its sensing faculties. Only ten percent of us think at this optimum frequency naturally. The rest of us need to be trained to do so.

INNER VOICE—FRIEND OR FOE?

The XYZ Corporation is on its collective toes. Everybody is waiting for the "go" command from the executive officer of the company. The feasibility study is a beauty. The most recent market analysis looks right on the money. Even the projections, at best illusionary figures, seem solid. All the ingredients for sound decision making are here and all point in the direction "go."

But that "go" command never comes. The executive officer has listened to another voice. Deep down inside within a mysterious chamber in his mind, something has whispered "no." "Let's hold off on this project," he tells his staff. "We have to concentrate on ongoing projects first."

Later, it turns out that a better approach to the project has been developed. Intuition wins again.

This executive was one of the ten percent. He had developed the ability to listen to his inner feelings, otherwise known as gut feelings, intuition, or perception. Some prefer to call him "lucky."

J.P. Morgan was "lucky." One of the greatest business tycoons of this country, he was known to visit fortune tellers to become more effective in hearing his intuitive voice. Another giant of American business, Cornelius Vanderbilt, consulted clairvoyants.

A test was conducted at Rutgers University some years ago in which businessmen were pitted against computers.

The men were asked to predict what number would come up next from the computer which was programmed to produce random numbers. The businessmen who headed successful businesses did far better than the other less successful businessmen. When confronted with the results, the successful businessmen admitted that they often ignored expensive engineering, marketing, or consultants' reports and made decisions on instinct. "Don't tell my stockholders."

To business executives educated in scientifically oriented management techniques, "hunch" and "gut feeling" are dirty words, as bad as ESP, psychic, or clairvoyant. But, we are emerging from the dark ages. Business is now showing its respect and even seeking for ways to amplify that inner voice.

TRAINING THAT INNER VOICE

The Silva Method is tried and true. Four million graduates of the training can attest to its successful use in business and in private life.

The Executive Thirty-Hour Silva Method Course is for developing executives to be clairvoyants. It is taught in three full days, or the equivalent thereof, usually over a three-day weekend—anywhere in the United States where a group requests it. This book is both a backup textbook for the Course and a manual for business managers and executives who wish to enhance their intuitive and clairvoyant capabilities independently.

Reading is objective. It instructs you to train yourself to function subjectively. It does not train you the way attending a course trains you. But, if a business executive or manager conscientiously follows the instructions in this book, a new dimension in thinking will be developed—a subjective dimension—and that means a new dimension for solving problems, making sound decisions, and performing effectively.

The Executive Thirty-Hour Course is concentrated. It can produce clairvoyant executives in three days only because of the presence of a skilled trainer able to lead you through the subjective experiences that activate right brain functioning. Using this book, the time element must of necessity be less concentrated.

You are leading yourself through subjective experiences, following instructions you have just read. This requires one small step at a time, or more specifically, five to fifteen minutes a day. The total amount of self-training is about the same as that required for the intensive training in total elapsed training time, but now that time, in these smaller increments, is spread over a larger period, and the three days become about fifty days.

Some executives may take longer; some may be able to shorten the time. All will acquire new skills, which will begin to emerge long before those training days are completed, and which will make the time invested a minuscule expense for the professional and business benefits that result.

For those business executives and managers who expect to take the Thirty-Hour Course, are taking it, or have already taken it, this book provides an introduction, course textbook, and reinforcement manual combined.

Man was once intuitive. The complexities of the objective civilized world have suppressed that ability. The Silva Method restores that ability. For most of us, it is a new way of thinking—genius-like, incredible, superhuman. For all of us, it is using more of the mind for business and personal success.

AMPLIFYING THE INNER VOICE

An editor of a national women's magazine states, "When I read a manuscript . . . only intuition can say this is truth, readers will like it." She calls this "secret personal knowledge."

Dr. Jonas Salk, developer of the polio vaccine, says, "Intuition is something we don't understand the biology of yet. But it is always with excitement that I wake up in the morning wondering what my intuition will toss up to me, like gifts from the sea. I work with it, and rely upon it. It's my partner."

Another scientist likened intuition to "cosmic fishing." "You feel a nibble. Then you've got to hook the fish."

Unfortunately, too many of us "fishermen" ignore the nibble. We get a hunch, light a cigarette, and forget it.

Precisely how the mind puts things together is currently being charted. We are beginning to know more about how the brain retrieves fragments of knowledge from the subconscious memory banks of neurons and fuses them instantly with new information. But what continues to elude researchers is just how the brain utilizes information not stored in those neurons—information at a distance, or information that has not taken place yet. We can only accept for now that the right brain functions in a timeless, spaceless realm, and then go about using it, profitably.

The first thing we need to do is to go within, where the voice is located; in effect, analyzing it. This process of going within is called meditation.

Meditation can be passive, where you relax blissfully in the joy of the inner self. This is what is generally understood by the term meditation. It can also be active, or dynamic. This is where you relax blissfully as before but then use your imagination in some creative way. This is when the intuition is activated to provide answers and to solve problems.

India is a poverty-ridden country engulfed in problems. Yet, India is the source spring of meditation. India's meditative techniques are passive. In 1981, my writing associate, Dr. Stone, went to Adyar, India, at the invitation of the Theosophical Society whose international headquarters is located there. He was asked to teach dynamic meditation.

One would think it would be like "carrying coals to Newcastle" for a westerner to teach meditation in India. However, using the mind in meditation to solve problems was a new concept in India. His lectures were increasingly attended.

Now that visit has been followed up by other Silva Method lecturers. Classes in many parts of Asia are breaking attendance records. It is to be hoped that the problem-ridden countries of the world will activate intuition to help solve them. That is already under way with a Silva Method "explosion" in Central and South America.

The business manager is a problem-ridden microcosm. He needs to begin the amplification of the intuitive voice, first by learning passive meditation, and then by extending that state into dynamic meditation.

SCREENING OUT STRESS

They say that an apple a day will keep the doctor away. Whether or not apples are in season, try meditation to "keep the doctor away" by refreshing your physical self. The simple act of getting comfortable in a chair, closing your eyes, and taking a deep breath is a boon to every cell of your body—the brain included. But when you deepen that relaxation—and the method is just as simple—every vital organ is able to rejuvenate itself.

The physical health of the body is prima facie evidence of the well-being of the brain. The brain runs the body. The stress of the Beta world, the world of your human relations at home or in business, is killing.

Doctors used to think that half of all diseases were psycho-somatic; that is, mind affecting body. The effect of emotions, attitudes, and feelings were making us sick. Today, the medical profession accepts a figure closer to 100 percent and maybe by the time this page reaches your eyes, that figure will be reached.

Cancer is one of the "holdouts" but recent research shows that stress causes cancer to worsen and spread in laboratory animals. Vernon Riley, chairman of the microbiology department at Pacific Northwest Research Foundation, was quoted in the press as saying that there is a dramatically higher percentage of new cancer growth when mice are placed under laboratory stress, which casts doubt on past studies using mice, because the increased cancer was attributed to substances being tested when it may have actually resulted from laboratory stress.

Yes, people can get sick from stress. Certainly, stress depletes you. Prolonged stress has been found to reduce the white blood cell count. That means resistance goes down.

This translates into: You can get a headache from that deadline you are working against. You can get ulcers from the upcoming job cutback. You can get the flu because of that new supervisor—unless you are able to screen out stress.

Sitting comfortably in a chair, closing your eyes, and taking a deep breath is the way to begin, but there is more.

DEFUSING STRESS WITH MEDITATION

Meditation is the first step in the Silva Method. When you meditate, you go to Alpha. At Alpha you are stress-free.

There is no way to bring fear, anxiety, or animosity with you to Alpha; that is Beta "stuff." If those feelings are present, they will anchor you in Beta. If they intrude at Alpha, you will be ending your meditation.

So, Alpha is a stress-free state. Is it any wonder that your body "eats it up"?

How do you meditate? There are many ways to do it. Music, mantras, chants, gongs, incense—all are helpful aids to meditation, but not exactly appropriate for the business executive.

The Silva Method *is* appropriate for managers and executives because it does not introduce any devices. It uses the mind to mind itself.

It supplies a simple, natural method to first relax the body and to then relax the mind. It needs to be in that order because if the body is not relaxed, it is like an attention-demanding child. It does not permit the mind to relax: tight belt; uncomfortable chair; shoes pinch; give me this, give me that.

So, first you relax the body, then the mind. It is not easy to relax the body or the mind in the middle of the day. You are going to learn to do this first at the easiest time of day—when you first wake up. It will then be an easy matter to use your skill to recreate the relaxed experience any time you wish.

Why will you wish it? Because you will enjoy the feeling. You will find out that your body responds, you feel healthier, your levels of energy improve, and you function better as a manager. This will be just a smaller part of bigger and better advantages to come—like avoiding burnout; like becoming a genius.

HOW TO MEDITATE

I am now going to give you the initial steps to get in control of the Alpha level. This is where you must start your training. From this page on are instructions you must carry out even before you do the procedures which you have already read about in the previous chapters, and those which will come later.

When you awake in the morning, go to the bathroom, if you have to, then get back into bed. Close your eyes, and roll them slightly upward (about 20 degrees). Now, count backwards slowly from 100 to one. Do not count out loud; count mentally to yourself. Count slowly, waiting about one second between numbers. Feel yourself going deeper and deeper within.

When you reach the count of one, you would be ready to program yourself for specific benefits and to release your imagination for problem solving; but this must wait until you practice more. Instead, enjoy the blissful, serene state for a few minutes. Then use the coming-out procedure.

The Silva Method for coming out is to say mentally, "I am going to count from 1 to 5. When I reach the count of 5, I will open my eyes, feeling wide awake, feeling fine and in perfect health, feeling better than before. One, 2, 3 . . . When I open my eyes at the count of five, I will feel wide awake, in perfect health, better than before . . . 4, 5; eyes open; wide awake, better than before. And this is so."

That is all there is to it. But there are ways to go wrong and ways to get better results.

One way to go wrong is to attempt meditation if you are intoxicated, emotionally involved, or just hyperactive. Alpha is a longer way off when you are in a high Beta state such as this. Alpha is close by when you first awaken.

When you wake up and go to the bathroom, set your alarm clock for ten or fifteen minutes, in case you fall asleep. You will not have to do this after practicing and getting Alpha more under control.

Always use the same method of going in and coming out. After ten days, count only from 50 to 1. After ten more days, count only from 25 to 1, and after ten more days 10 to 1 will bring you to your Alpha level. Coming out remains 1 to 5. Open your eyes at the count of 5, no sooner, no later. The discipline is essential to controlling your mind.

When you have completed forty days of practice, the last ten counting down 10 to 1, you are ready to shorten the procedure to 5 to 1, and to begin using the Alpha level for a purpose, any purpose you desire.

So, you will have a 5-to-1 method to enter and a 1-to-5 method to come out of your meditating.

Once you become a passive meditator in the way described, you are able to become a dynamic meditator. That is the beginning of managerial benefits.

CHANGES DURING MEDITATION

"Nothing happened." "It was nice but I did not feel anything different." "I don't think I was meditating."

These are common reactions to the first experiences of meditation. You relax. You enjoy the peace. You end your relaxation. You are back where you started. This is not exactly so. Changes have occurred during your meditation that are measurable. We have already discussed the changes in your brain wave pattern—the slowing up of brain pulsations. Tests made on meditators at the Thorndike Memorial Laboratory, a part of the Harvard Medical Unit at Boston City Hospital, and also at the University of California at Irvine, showed that even novices slowed both their oxygen consumption and their carbon dioxide elimination considerably. The respiratory rate and the volume of air breathed declined. Blood pressure was lowered. Blood lactate concentration dropped, this being a measurement of anaerobic metabolism; that is, metabolism in the absence of free oxygen.

You do not monitor those physiological factors when you close your eyes and meditate. You are more inclined to look for changes in your awareness. Since you can still hear sounds, since you are still aware of where you are and what you are doing, since you can still think about this or that, you believe "nothing happened."

The meditative level is a natural state. You go into it daily when you daydream or relax. There is nothing weird about it.

No sirens go off when you reach it. There is no formal announcement. What you are doing is getting in control of it. Once you have meditation under control, you can use it for a purpose.

It may seem childish to practice something so simple for forty days, but each experience acts as a reference point for the next. That is why the procedure must be the same—place, time, methodology. Introducing variables slows progress.

As you practice, physiological benefits are occurring. Every cell of your body, every vital organ, all of the tissues and muscles, are celebrating your relaxation. They delight in it. They are able to use the hiatus from stress to restore themselves.

Being awake is stressful for the average person. It means being open to all the stressful thoughts of the work-a-day world, of things to be done, of human events to be dealt with.

When a large insurance company in Honolulu had much of its staff take the Silva Method training course, within two days a sixty-year-old man with crippling arthritis in his hands demonstrated to the class that he had regained full mobility in his fingers. In another class, a woman who warned the lecturer that she had colitis and might have to interrupt the meditations to go to the bathroom, reported that the colitis had disappeared. Headaches end, lower back pain is relieved, nerves become steady.

Nothing happened? No, bells did not ring. A voice did not say, "Welcome to the state of meditation." But you may have added to the length of your life.

BIOFEEDBACK AND MEDITATION TRAINING

S.P., manager of a branch bank, was convinced that his meditation was "going nowhere." He was plagued with the thought that others might be doing it but somehow it was escaping him. It was interfering with his confidence. It was suggested that he test himself on a small device called a galvanic skin reactor (GSR), a standard biofeedback device.

S.P. sat down at a table, placed two of his fingers on the

padded terminals, and turned it on. There was a beeping sound that could be adjusted from fast to slow. He adjusted it to the critical point between the two extremes. The moment S.P. closed his eyes and turned them slightly upward, there was an audible slowing down. This deceleration of the beeping sound continued during the countdown until it was definitely at a slower rate. When S.P. counted himself back up, the beeping sound accelerated back to its original faster rate. S.P. was all smiles. He had received "concrete" proof that he was "doing it."

The GSR measures the skin resistance changes that are brought about by differing levels of adrenalin in the blood. An excited person has less skin resistance due to a high level of adrenalin. A relaxed person has high skin resistance due to a lower level of adrenalin. The instrument detecting low skin resistance beeps at a fast rate. When the instrument detects high resistance, the beeps slow down. This is, of course, the principle of the polygraph, or lie detector.

Some disciplines and therapies use biofeedback devices as their main tool for learning. Patients learn how to lower their blood pressure, improve the heart rhythm, get rid of headaches and end many troublesome psychosomatic health problems with biofeedback devices.

Although Silva Method graduates do not require biofeedback equipment, many take advantage of its availability to take them beyond the basic training to deeper levels of mind and to reinforce their programming.

Available equipment goes beyond the simple device just described, which we call Trainer I, to more sophisticated trainers such as the Silva Educator. This device holds the first United States patent that makes use of the fact that human concentration turns on an educational program. This instrument turns on a motivational tape, or your own company's discourse, only when you reach your Alpha level—your most receptive state for concentration and learning.

Biofeedback equipment is always helpful but not necessary. It is not necessary to you at this point in your initial experiences with the Alpha level. What is necessary is that you accept your meditation as being meditation.

If you are worried about whether you are relaxing, you indeed have something to worry about—your worrying.

Worrying about relaxation is the ideal methodology to use to prevent relaxation. Worry is stress; the opposite of relaxation.

The best advice anyone can give you on this point is to accept that you are meditating, regardless of its depth. Be comfortable about being comfortable. Be relaxed about your relaxation. If you get "uptight" about relaxation, you are getting in your own way.

Do it. Enjoy it. Know that it gets better and better.

TIPS FOR DEEPENING MEDITATION

Based on the experience of others and the results of decades of research, here are some ideas for improving your initial experiences with meditation and accelerating your progress.

1. Eyes turned slightly upwards is an easy step to forget. But it is important. For reasons that we do not yet understand, turning the eyes slightly upward—at about twenty degrees above the horizontal plane of sight— triggers Alpha.

2. Take a moment now to refresh your memory of the feeling of "letting go." Make a fist. Tighten it. Tighten it more. Let go. The instant of letting go is the feeling of physical relaxation. Do it again with an ankle. With your jaw. It feels so good to "let go."

3. Before closing your eyes, tire them by staring at a spot on the ceiling about forty-five degrees above your normal plane of seeing. Try to keep from blinking. Do not turn your head up. Turn your eyes up, without lifting your head. When you feel you must blink, and certainly after no more than half a minute of staring, close your eyes and continue with your meditation in the usual way.

4. Before ending your meditation with the 1-to-5 countup, tell yourself mentally, "Each time I relax this way, I go deeper, faster."

FROM PASSIVE TO DYNAMIC MEDITATION

If you have too much to remember when you meditate, you could be making it more difficult to go from Beta to Alpha. You already have enough to do and you need to experience this procedure daily for forty days in order for it to become shorter and more automatic.

Each repetition is a reference point for the next time. The more reference points you have, the greater the facility and ease of meditating. It becomes familiar ground to you.

In forty days, when it is no longer strange for a busy person like you to take a few minutes of your valuable time to "do nothing," you are ready to make the transition from passive meditation to dynamic meditation.

At that time, picture objects familiar to you, preferably an object containing color.

You might select an orange or a lemon. You might picture a fresh, crisp head of lettuce, or a fresh, crisp hundred-dollar bill. Whatever object you decide on, hold it in your mind's eye for a few seconds. If it disappears, welcome to the club. We are all in the habit of jumping from one thing to another—remember that drunken monkey?—so do not get upset with yourself. Permit new thoughts to intrude like actors on a stage. But, since you are the playwright, let their roles take them offstage when they have had their say, and bring back the original picture.

Once this is working to your satisfaction, move to more complex images that involve not only color but some movement. Some suggestions might be:

- White clouds drifting across a beautiful blue sky

- Drops of morning dew on a sunlit rose, reflecting all the colors of the rainbow like diamonds

- A babbling brook

You are to visualize away from your body. Imagine the picture or scene to be "out there." If you visualize the picture or scene to be in the area of the eyes or eyelids, you are using biological senses—the eyes. Visualizing away from your body keeps you at Alpha. Seeing with the eyes brings you back to Beta. Normal vision is at Beta; visualizing is at Alpha.

HOW TO INCREASE YOUR VISUALIZING SKILL

Each time you position yourself comfortably in bed, close your eyes, turn them slightly upward and count backward from 5 to 1, spend a few minutes visualizing before bringing yourself up 1 to 5.

Visualization and imagination are two faculties that contribute to clairvoyance. You may feel that holding simple pictures in your mind is a waste of time. It smacks of daydreaming. Why picture this or that? This erroneous universal concept about visualization and imagination is the reason more people are not clairvoyant. The few minutes you spend visualizing each morning is activating idle brain neurons and putting them into harness to work for you—the right brain neurons. It is so important for the business executive to do this, that I am asking you to practice during the day as well as when you awaken.

During the day, while reading, stop at a word that you can relate to a past experience, and make a mental picture. For instance, if you read the word "house," stop and remember a house that you have seen and visualize it. Bring back a memory you have of that house. Do the same when you hear people talk. If the name of something is mentioned that you have seen in the past and you can convert it to a mental image, do so. Next, extend those mental images into scenes— like mental movies.

ONE IMPORTANT MENTAL IMAGE

Dynamic meditation is creative. It programs you and it programs other people. It programs events. The pictures you put on your mental screen are shadows of things to come.

Stop for a moment. Haven't you been doing this right

along—visualizing? Everybody does, business managers included. What do you visualize? You picture your problems. You worry. You worry about your status, your quotas, your deadlines, your obstacles, your problems. What are you really doing to those problems as you sit quietly picturing them with your visualization? You're reinforcing them.

With the Silva Method, you no longer think in terms of problems. You think in terms of solutions. What a turnaround takes place!

Since you are involved in the picture, you need to begin to visualize yourself in practice sessions.

A woman looks in a mirror when she fixes her hair, but does not really pay attention to the whole visual image. Similarly, a man looks in a mirror when he shaves and combs his hair, but takes his visual image for granted.

As a result, you are likely to find it easier to picture an orange than to picture yourself. Here is how to correct this. Look in the mirror. Memorize your face. Close your eyes, turn them slightly upward, and put yourself on your mental screen. Open your eyes to see how well you did. Close them again and repeat the image. Do this several times until you are satisfied that you are able to "see" yourself.

REALISTIC IMAGERY

Some people are able to picture in great detail and in color, naturally. This is an excellent start toward becoming clairvoyant. But it is not essential. As you begin to visualize daily, you get better and better.

What is essential is having the concept of something. Then the picture follows naturally. Close your eyes now, turn them slightly upward and picture a whole green watermelon being cut in half so that you can see inside . . .

What did you see besides the green of the outside? You probably saw the red meat, the black seeds, perhaps the white inside rind. But I did not ask you to see that. You saw it automatically because of your memory of the entire concept of "watermelon." If you had never seen a watermelon before, you would be in trouble with that picture. But because you have seen a watermelon, the details of the picture popped right into your mind.

Try not to picture this. Do not visualize a white polar bear in a pink bikini. Did I hear you laugh? You had no way of keeping the concept from being pictured by your mind. Now picture this: a borkle. No picture? Why? Because there is no such thing and therefore you had no concept to picture.

Do not become concerned that you are not visualizing in "wide screen technicolor." Just as you are relaxed about relaxing, be relaxed about visualizing. Accept the degree to which you are able to visualize.

The images you are making are creative. And they get better and better.

YOU AND CREATIVE IMAGERY

How do you picture yourself in your meditation? Should you picture yourself on your mental screen fixing your hair? In these days of shortage, why waste energy?

See yourself as you wish to be. These are just practice sessions, but the energy you are putting out with your Alpha visualizing is real, creative energy. Is there some aspect of yourself that you would like to improve? Select a scene in which you are exhibiting that improvement.

One manager knew he was being too abrupt with his people. Although he knew this, he could not change. That was the way he was. He decided to use in his meditations a picture of himself smiling, nodding his head, and listening patiently. Within a week, he was doing exactly that and was getting warm consideration back from his formerly indifferent employees.

If there is no particular trait you want to work on, use a goal that you would like to reach. Hold a picture of yourself with that goal attained.

A manager on the night shift wanted to work days instead. He used a picture of himself on the job in daylight hours with the sun streaming through the windows. It took three weeks, and the picture was realized.

How? As we continue, you will understand more about this creative energy and how it transcends space and reaches minds wherever it must in order to solve the problem or reach the goal.

If you have no particular trait to work on and no specific

goal to attain at this time, use a picture of yourself in some symbolic setting that signifies success for you:

- Seated behind a huge desk indicating an important position

- Living in a larger home

- Seated on the platform at a testimonial dinner for you

- Conferring with VIPs

Be careful of the picture you select. You had better want it. Each Alpha visualizing session in your meditation brings that picture closer to reality.

Are you ready to become a visionary?

6

Enhanced Memory and Concentration for Effective Management

A business development of the past ten years is the birth of the businessman/philosopher. Because business success depends largely on the ability to perceive social change and trends, businessmen are getting together more and more and talking about public issues. In 1972, SRI issued a report entitled *Changing Image of Man*. It urged companies to be aware of an emerging business and social ethic characterized by concern for spirituality and the quality of life, and to move with the times.

An example of a business moving with the times is Hoffman-LaRoche, the pharmaceutical company I mentioned before. Despite its commitment to allopathic medicine, it began distributing tapes to physicians, free of charge, on holistic approaches to healing. It also sponsored symposia on alternative therapies. The company is now building a plant to manufacture Vitamin C—still scorned by most doctors.

The Silva Method conditioning cycles include the following statement which, when accepted by the student, becomes programming; that is, it becomes part of that person's lifestyle:

You will continue to strive to take part in constructive and creative activities to make this a better world to live in, so that when we move on we shall have left behind a better world for those who follow.

Now, this might sound like an admirable, unselfish, altruistic statement to make. But it is really quite selfish and practical. If you do not believe so, try programming yourself with that statement during your daily Alpha practice sessions. As you respond to the programming and strive to make this a better world to live in, good things will begin to happen to you. You will grow and prosper.

I applaud the new breed of businessmen/philosophers. They are thinking in terms of the bigger picture. They are visionaries. Their companies will grow and prosper. May their tribe increase.

INTERIM PROGRESS REPORT

The Silva Method for getting in control of your mind and having more of it work for you is comprised of reading and doing.

You will read to acquire understanding—left brain progress; and then practice pursuant to the instructions—right brain progress. Your reading may outdistance your practice; no problem. It certainly takes less time to read (days) and more time to practice (weeks). You may want to use two book marks, one to flag how far you have progressed in reading, the other how far you have progressed in activating more of your mind to work for you through practice.

Let us review the left brain and right brain progress so far.

Left Brain Progress

- Meditation slows the brain waves to the Alpha rhythm.
- At Alpha, the right brain is activated.
- The Silva Method is a way to control your brain at Alpha.
- By relaxing and visualizing you are exercising that control.
- Visualizing and/or affirming at Alpha constitute programming.
- Programming can cancel unwanted behavior, increase skills, and trigger problem solving.
- Desire, expectation and belief are the "on" switch, voltage, and power needed for successful programming.

- Successful programming can cause the brain to function intuitively and psychically.
- Meditation causes brain and body changes measurable by biofeedback.
- Applications for business managers run the gamut of activities and responsibilities, from handling stress to amplifying intuition.
- The Silva Method is producing super managers.

Right Brain Progress

- To begin, practice passive meditation when awakening in the morning. Lie comfortably, close eyes, and turn them slightly upward. Then count backward from 100 to 1. Then end by counting from 1 to 5, affirming before counting at the count of 3, and again when opening the eyes at the count of 5, "I am wide awake, feeling great."
- At the end of a ten-day period, shorten the count progressively; first 50 to 1, then 25 to 1, then 10 to 1, then 5 to 1. There will be 50 days of morning practice.
- Before coming out, tell yourself mentally, "Each time I relax this way, I go deeper, faster."
- Begin dynamic meditation by visualizing colorful objects, then advance with natural scenes, putting yourself in the picture.
- When reading a book or listening to people talk, make mental images of objects brought up, using pertinent memories.

MAGIC OF MENTAL PICTURES

Centuries of esoteric and metaphysical literature have insisted that "thoughts are things." Now science is examining in the laboratory how thoughts are indeed creative energy at work.

A person affects the shape of crystals forming in a supersaturated solution. "I'm going to create twin towers. Now I will add to the left tower but not to the right." And he does.

A person affects photographic film. "I am going to create a

picture of a church." The camera is held to his head and snapped. The film is developed. The image is there.

A scientist accepts a Nobel prize for discovering a subatomic particle. In accepting, he publicly states, "I wonder if that particle was there before I started looking for it."

The definition of the scientific approach as an objective discipline has gone down the drain. Scientists are now considered to be a variable in their own experiments. What they visualize happening can influence the outcome.

A 707 bound from Los Angeles to Honolulu could not lower its landing gear on arrival. Foam was spread, a safe belly landing was made, and the passengers slid to safety. It was then pointed out that the movie shown on the flight contained that identical incident. Could some 200 passengers, relaxed and picturing such a problem, create it?

Reverend Norman Vincent Peale has been encouraging people to think positively.* He says that our thoughts affect our lives. He gives scores of examples of how negative thoughts produce failure patterns and positive thoughts produce success patterns. His books have sold in the millions, because the basic premise is sound. It works.

It works because our brain neurons are programmed for solutions and survival. We interfere by thinking in terms of problems and limited modes of survival—limited intelligence, limited health, limited love, limited money, limited experiences, limited production, limited success.

When you stop limiting your thoughts, you free your brain neurons to move you—and others with whom you are in touch—to new horizons.

MEASURABLE EFFECTS OF MENTAL PICTURES

Do this simple test: Hold your arms out horizontally in front of you. Close your eyes. Picture a shopping bag over the right wrist filled to the brim with recognizable groceries. Feel the weight. A red balloon filled with helium is tied around

---

The Power of Positive Thinking, Prentice-Hall, Inc., Englewood Cliffs, N.J.

your left wrist. Feel it tug upward. After a moment open your eyes and look at your arms.

Put the book down and do it now.

When you opened your eyes and looked at your arms, one was likely lower than the other. Usually, it is the right arm that is lower, having reacted to the imaged weight. However, sometimes we feel the motion and overcorrect, causing the right arm to be higher. Either way, the mental image affected the physical body.

Here is another simple test: Go to your alpha level in the prescribed way. Picture a lemon. Imagine you are cutting the lemon in half with a knife. Now imagine you are biting into the lemon. End your session in the prescribed way.

Even reading these instructions is likely to cause your mouth to water. Mental pictures affect even those parts of our body that are not under conscious control.

Athletes are beginning to realize the importance of mental pictures in their performance. Golfers, runners, tennis players are improving through pictures of perfection.

Recently a junior high school boys' physical education class, which was about to begin the basketball season, was divided into two groups and tested for accuracy in foul shooting. One group then practiced daily in the gymnasium. The other group practiced at home in their living rooms, picturing themselves making perfect foul shots. At the end of the period, each group was again tested in the gymnasium shooting fouls. Each group had improved by the same amount. Mental imagery was as good as physical activity in improving the skill.

MENTAL PICTURES HINDER OR HELP

Get a wastebasket and a small ball. Sit far enough away so that if you try to toss the ball into the basket, you may miss some of the time, and get the ball in some of the time. Throw a few to make sure you are far enough away.

Now remember one time when you missed. Remember just what happened to the ball, "see" its trajectory away from the basket. Hold this memory in your mind as you throw ten more balls. Remember how many times you missed.

Change your memory picture to the most recent toss that was a perfect hit. Hold that memory picture as you throw ten more balls. Your score should have improved.

In the Silva Method training course, we do not toss balls into baskets. We use our mental images in controlled ways to create positive changes and develop creative solutions.

Would you like to play some more games? Would you like to hold failure images in your mind as you play the "game" of personnel relationships? Production control? Safety? Decision making? Most definitely you would not. Intuitively, you know what the penalty for that would be.

Images are a right brain activity. They are the causal realm. Therefore they are creative. Discover the power of imaging and it's like discovering a long-lost wealthy uncle.

IMAGING FOR BETTER MEMORY

Suppose you had ten shops, A through J, and each needed a different tool, supply item, or raw material. How long would it take for you to memorize these requirements? You would write them down, of course, but memory is often needed on the job. We are going to assume that memory is needed now. Make a list of ten items, lettered A to J. A=Light bulbs, B=Cleaner, etc. Then memorize it, testing yourself, and stop the watch only when you have been able to name all the letters and objects correctly. Par is about ten minutes.

Memorizing is a left brain–dominated activity. Now let's try a right brain–dominated activity—visualizing. To picture vividly, we need to translate the letters into objects. Then we can use objects as pegs on which to hang the shop items.

One simple way to translate letters into pictures is to use animals. Make another list:

A	Ant	Light bulbs	F	Fox	etc.
B	Buffalo	Cleaner	G	Giraffe	etc.
C	Cat	etc.	H	Horse	etc.
D	Dog	etc.	I	Iguana	etc.
E	Elephant	etc.	J	Jaguar	etc.

When I say "go," you will again time yourself, but now you

will not memorize. Instead of memorizing, you will make a picture in your mind that uses lightbulbs and ants. Next you will make a picture that connects cleaner with buffalo. Perhaps you see ants running all over the light bulbs. Perhaps you see a buffalo being scrubbed down with industrial cleaner. Any picture you make that physically connects the shop item with the animal is fine.

What is important is that you pause and make the picture. "Ants running all over the lightbulbs" is not a picture. It is a string of words. You must not use words. You must stop and make a mental picture. Your decision to use a buffalo being cleaned is not sufficient. You must see it happening.

Have you made your list? Are you ready to make the mental picture? Take your time. Make the pictures real.

Go . . .

Now cover the objects on your list and look only at the animals. Picture the ants. Immediately you see the bulbs, etc. You should be correct the first time around. Elapsed time: about one minute.

MEMORY VIA THE SILVA METHOD

If remembering long lists of items is part of your job, you might want to adopt a system of memory pegs. You can use the alphabet-animal system outlined above; you can design your own pictorial system; or you can study the Dr. Bruno Furst Memory Peg System* which we recommend.

Be that as it may, you are already acquiring a better memory, by doing your meditation exercises. As you move from passive meditation to active meditation, your use of mental imagery is reinforcing memory. You can recall an entire scene to remember something, and that something will be there in that scene.

You are now practicing your meditation for a few minutes daily. You are seeing yourself in positive, goal-reaching, solution pictures. The more dynamic meditation you do, the

---

The Practical Way To A Better Memory, Fawcett World Library, N.Y.

better your memory. Picturing automatically enhances memory; and much more.

YOU CAN RAISE YOUR INTELLIGENCE LEVEL

When you activate the right hemisphere of the brain with Alpha picturing—dynamic meditation—you have more of your mind working for you. When you have more of your mind working for you, your intelligence level goes up. Measures such as Intelligence Quotient (I.Q.) by definition go up.

Intelligence is a bicameral activity. Both the left and right hemispheres of the brain are used. In the past, brain science and psychology have looked at the feeling system of the right brain and the intellectual system of the left brain as two separate and distinct systems.

Now, systems scientist Paul LaViolette and psychiatrist William Gray have proposed a new theory of brain function that sees left brain logical thinking and right brain feeling as integrated in the learning and creative problem-solving process. Feelings, they say, form patterns that screen information. With the help of feelings, the mind can better organize and reorganize its information.

As business managers go to the Alpha level and picture solutions, they are activating the right—feeling—hemisphere. They become more intelligent, as measured by their problem-solving ability.

EFFECTS OF ALPHA ON LEARNING

When I started my research in Laredo, Texas in 1944, my goal was to challenge the then-accepted fact that a person's so-called I.Q. never fluctuates by more than a few points in either direction. I knew then that education had overlooked an important area: subjective learning. I felt that with subjective learning, we might make important changes in intelligence levels.

I began by training my own children with subjective functioning. This meant providing a tension-free atmosphere. We were ahead of the game right there. I continued by providing positive statements that counteracted the fear and limitation programming unwittingly induced by the teachers. Additional positive programming then eliminated distractions while studying and reinforced good study habits.

All this was happening at the Alpha level, and with the use of positive statements and positive mental images. I knew we were using subjective methods that reached more deeply within the subconscious. What I did not know was that I was helping my children to activate their right brains. The functions of the two hemispheres were not fully known at that time.

My children improved in their schoolwork, so much so that neighbors asked me to do the same for their children. This gave me more subjects for my research.

Something else happened that stunned me. A strange pattern began to emerge. I would test the children on their homework. The children started answering questions before I asked them. At first, this seemed like a coincidence. But as it happened again and again, I became aware that it was more than chance. Both the boys and the girls would answer questions that I was about to ask.

The children had become sensitive in a new way. They were sensing information psychically. They would tell me an answer to a question before I asked it. ("Why did you tell me that? I did not ask you." "I guessed you would ask.") They would tell me the end of a story before I finished reading it.

I had started the research with the raising of the I.Q. as my goal. I had answered that question, but I had raised many more, some of which are still unanswered.

EFFECTS ON THE UTILIZATION OF LEARNING

Twenty-eight years later, in September, 1972, a group of Mind Control lecturers gathered in Philadelphia to teach the Silva Method to 2,000 girls of Hallahan High School. Other schools had successfully completed the training, but the special significance of this project was to measure the personality growth and maturing effect. Standardized testing procedures were used before and after.

The first and greatest change was in an area that psychologists call "ego strength." The term is used to describe a person who thinks for himself, determines what his goals are, and has the courage to say what he feels; as opposed to the person who goes along with the crowd and depends on others for ideas and decisions. There was a dramatic growth in "ego strength."

The second most dramatic change came in the area of reduced anxiety. The students became more settled, calmer and self-assured. Other changes for the better included social confidence, social awareness, and more steadiness of purpose.

These were positive results. They pointed to enhanced synthesis of the educational experience—a maturing of the individual.

Can similar results be obtained with grown people? A clear answer was obtained in a test made with forty-one adults on welfare conducted in Ottawa County in western Michigan. A low self-concept was the common denominator of this group, whether it led to being on welfare or whether it was caused by being on welfare.

With the Silva Method, a dramatic change took place. It could occur by chance only once in one hundred thousand times. Not only did self-concept improve, but a sense of realism about that improved self-concept was also acquired. These adults also showed a movement toward greater control, balance, and growth. Moral ability and religious commitment were brought more into everyday practice. The group became more ethical and trustworthy.

Are you practicing your dynamic meditation daily, Mr. or Ms. Business Manager?

HOW TO TRIGGER THE BRAIN

When you have completed more than ten weeks of practice, several in dynamic meditation, you will reach a state where more and more techniques can be used by you in your managerial responsibilities such as those set forth in the first three chapters. These weeks of practice have put you in touch with your mind. Your mind is delighted. "Where have you been all my life?" ask the brain neurons, especially those in the right brain, as they are finally able to get into the ball game.

You have established communications with your mind. It is able to tell you things you have been blocking out. You are able to give it requests that it will now fulfill. One such request can be to have a deeper level of awareness. That is almost like the child who, when greeted by a department store Santa Claus and told he could have one wish, replied, "My one wish is to have ten wishes."

If you can get your mind to function for you at a deeper level of awareness, you are able to concentrate better, recall what you read or hear better, be in the right place at the right time, and say the right thing.

A request to your mind needs to have a triggering device. In other words, you program that "when I do something, my mind does something." What you do is then the triggering device.

Standing on your head might be a triggering device, but that might not go over too well on the job. Sticking your finger in your ear might be adopted as the "signal" for your brain to function at a deeper level of awareness; but, again, this may be considered to be antisocial.

In the Silva Method, we use putting three fingers together of either hand—the first two fingers and thumb. We program that every time we do this our mind functions at a deeper level of awareness.

You can begin to use this triggering device yourself now. Include this in your dynamic meditation. Here is how:

• When you have closed your eyes, turned them slightly upward and counted backward from 5 to 1, put three fingers together of either hand, and repeat mentally, "Every time I put these three fingers together of either hand, my mind functions at a deeper level of awareness to accomplish whatever I desire."

Repeat this procedure for a week in dynamic meditation practice sessions. You will then be able to use it. Some applications might be:

– When you need to remember something

– When you need to participate in a meeting

– When you have a decision to make

– When you are on an inspection tour

– When you have a report to write or an important letter to answer

– When you are having an important telephone conversation

Other applications are provided in the initial chapters of this book.

As you use the Three Fingers Technique, it gets more and more successful. The programming is reinforced. Your expectation and belief rise.

THE SILVA METHOD IN A BOOK

The Silva Method is not "book learning." It is subjective experiencing. It takes practice. You must practice for seven weeks before you can be sure you are at the Alpha level. You must practice the Three Fingers Technique for seven days to make it work most effectively. There is another way to practice that can save time: You can be your own lecturer.

THE MANAGER'S PRIVATE INSTRUCTOR

You can make tapes for a number of purposes, and for combined purposes. For instance, you can give yourself a relaxation, or a programming, or a combined relaxation/programming. You can also make a tape of a complicated new operating procedure or other matter that you wish to learn, then play the tape while you are at the Alpha level.

You can talk to the cassette as if it were you. You can give yourself instructions to close your eyes, turn them slightly upward, take a deep breath. You can count backwards from 100 to 1, or from 10 to 1, or 5 to 1. You can ask yourself to be aware of your toes and relax your toes, then your ankles, feet, legs, knees, thighs, and hips. You can name all the parts of your body, instructing yourself to be aware of these parts and to relax them, all the way up to your scalp. You can ask yourself to picture natural scenes to induce a relaxed mind.

You can extend this to a programming tape to reinforce Silva Method programming. Ask yourself to see yourself improved in some particular way. If the tape is to be used as your regular morning meditation, see the day progress hour by hour the way you want it to—people working efficiently and in harmony, your being effective, the work getting done with time to spare. Lead yourself on the tape through such a mental "movie."

End the tape with some positive statements, including perhaps, "Each time I relax this way I go deeper, faster." Finally, bring yourself back up with the 1-to-5 count, "feeling great when you open your eyes, ready to create a successful day!"

If there is a long report or document you wish to learn, read it while recording. Make it a separate tape. You may want to introduce it with a relaxation similar to the previous tape. Without such an introduction, you may slip out of Alpha into Beta when you want to turn on the tape recorder.

Listen to the material at Alpha. Your mind will absorb it and recall will be easier. Listen to it again at Alpha a day or two later and you will know it as if you had memorized it.

THE PERCEIVED WORLD, THE REAL WORLD

In school we are told to study hard. Yet learning comes more readily when we are relaxed. We are told to cram for the exam. Yet, when we are free from this kind of anxiety and tension, we do better. "It's just your imagination," we are reprimanded. Yet, imagination is creative.

We live in a world different from the one we perceive. See that green wall? We call that a green wall, but it is really not green. We call it green because the light that has rebounded from it and entered our eyes is green. The wall has absorbed the whole spectrum of white light with the exception of the green which is reflected back to our eyes. Actually, the wall is every color except green. All of the colors reside in the wall except green, the only color the wall does not accept.

The perceived world is a material world. Matter is solid. Yet, behind this solid illusion is the atom with as much space between its nucleus and the electrons rotating around it, as there is space, relatively speaking, between the sun and the planets. Matter is just as penetrable as space.

Gradually, as our minds expand, as both hemispheres begin to function for us, we begin to see behind the illusions of the perceived world. We begin to function in the real world of energy and intelligence. We are no longer limited by past conditioning. We are no longer limited by I.Q.s, bank balances, and past experiences. We are no longer limited by our senses. We are able to rise above the time and space limitations of this perceived world and function mentally in genius-like ways.

Consciousness and thought are energy. Where they go, energy goes.

A manager of a credit agency goes over new accounts before assigning them to a field man. He goes to his Alpha level and, for each in turn, sees a check in full payment arriving.

"Usually it arrives within three days," he said. "If it does not arrive, it turns out that the person or company is bankrupt. In that case, a new client shows up and gives me more new business to make up for the loss."

Our brains appear to be separated by flesh, bone, skin and distance. But they resonate with each other when solutions to problems are desired. It is as if you and I are each connected to a Larger Intelligence, greater than the sum of its parts.

You resonate better with Larger Intelligence when you go beyond limited logical left brain thinking and permit both hemispheres to function. Why? Because your right hemisphere is your "connection." It is based in the creative realm—the causal world. It works for you in super ways because it has "connections."

In this chapter you have been given additional right brain activating steps to take:

- Use images for memory and clairvoyance.

- Program the Three Fingers technique for deeper awareness.

- Tape for wider programming uses.

Left brain *reading*, as interesting, absorbing and entertaining as it may be, will get you nowhere. Right brain *doing* will get you everywhere.

7

Silva Mind Control for a Successful Day

Visualization and imagination lead to clairvoyance. In the previous chapter, you began the practice of visualization. In this chapter, you begin the practice of imagination.

What is the difference? With visualization, we draw on memory; we recall scenes from the past. With imagination, we create scenes for the first time. The process of imagination opens mental channels for ingenuity, inspiration, and creativity.

It took you fifty days of morning practice to get to Alpha level under your control. Additional days have been spent practicing visualization as a prerequisite for imagination.

We have found a large variance in the number of practice sessions required by individuals to acquire satisfactory visualizing skills. It depends on how you have been using your mind in the past. So, we will not stipulate a definite number of morning practice sessions for visualization. When you feel that you are able to remember past events and "see" them as mental movies, you are ready to create new events and "see" them as mental movies.

Practice sessions now become more than practice sessions. Practice sessions now become creative. You have introduced pictures of yourself, improved in some way, in visualization practice sessions. These, too, are creative. These images are of new circumstances, unless you were equally successful in the past and were merely recalling that success. The reaching of a goal not reached before is a new image. So, to the extent that you have been using new pictures instead of memories, you have already begun to practice the use of imagination.

We are going to continue that practice now. But we are going to use mental movies that bear more on the present than on the future. We are going to use our imagination to create a perfect today. You will be able to see the results of your practice day by day, as the days get better and better.

New movies have "grand openings." Yours will, too.

AN INGREDIENT THAT MEANS BUSINESS

M.S., head of a Texas tool company, insisted that his key personnel take the Silva Method training course, on a shared cost basis. He also made the training a requirement for employment of new job applicants. All key sales personnel were included. Soon, half of his staff were Silva graduates.

There was resistance along the way. One man, who was getting nowhere in his job, said, "You're wasting your money. I can't sit for a whole day." M.S. pulled no punches. "Take the training or I'll be disappointed in you." The man knew what M.S. meant and agreed.

"He went from being totally negative to being totally positive before the training was half over," says M.S. "Shortly after, he used the Silva Method and landed a contract for us with the military to repair a base."

Overall, M.S. estimates that his company's sales increased "manifold" with the recalcitrant graduate increasing his sales 100-fold within two months.

Can you identify the element responsible for this sales promotion? You know it was not a new technical brochure, a new sales pitch, increased advertising, media publicity, or a direct mail campaign. Yet, in a way, it was all of these. Sales promotion involves communicating motivational information to the potential buyer. The Silva Method does exactly that. But it uses a different channel of communication than these standard sales promotion methods. It uses subjective communication.

A NEW MEDIUM OF COMMUNICATION

Subjective communication requires the use of the imagination. As you practice the use of the imagination—and I will now give ways to do that—mental "movies" involving your relations with other people get through to those people.

If your left brain is saying "hold it a minute," I am not surprised. You have never been taught that the imagination has anything at all to do with reality, much less that it creates it. "It is just your imagination." You heard this at a young age, repeatedly.

Mental "movies," at the Alpha level, are a real method of communicating. It is not "just your imagination."

I discussed this earlier. You may have also read of the work of Cleve Backster, who, with the aid of the polygraph, has been able to demonstrate repeatedly that this subjective communication is also going on between plants, between plants and humans, and even between single-celled organisms.*

If your left brain demands a scientific explanation, it is going to have to wait. Science has taken many years to accept the fact that "supernormal" powers of the mind exist. Now that they recognize what we can do, it is going to take even more years to explain what is happening.

We talk about our logical, intellectual, and reasoning abilities as the result of using our grey matter. Now a University of Pennsylvania team of psychologists has found anatomical differences in the two halves of our brain. The left brain, the analytical, has more grey matter. The right brain, intuitive, has more white matter.

Grey matter consists primarily of junctions and connections between brain cells. White matter consists mostly of nerve fibers, like wires.

The psychologists have concluded that left brain functioning needs more signal processing within tiny regions. Right brain functioning needs less processing, with signals carried over larger brain distances.

That's the beginning. Between the time of writing this and your reading this, there will undoubtedly be more findings toward and explanation of the right brain's ability to communicate subjectively.

When you use subjective communication, and experience the undeniable results, you begin to care less about

---

*"Evidence of a Primary Perception in Plant Life," *International Journal of Parapsychology*, 1968, Vol. 10. Also, *Secret Life of Plants*.

logical explanations and more about practical uses in your business.

SUCCESSFUL USE BREEDS MORE SUCCESS

An insurance executive took the Silva Method training course for the sole purpose of increasing his sales. Soon after completing it, he phoned us in Laredo, Texas to relate the following situation. He had approached a wealthy businessman in his community in order to sell him an education policy for his two teenage children. The businessman seemed receptive. The price was no problem. But somehow the insurance man was not able to get the information across sufficiently well to clinch the sale. He began to apply the usual sales pressure, visiting the businessman a number of times, until it got to the point where the secretary would lie and say her boss was not in.

The reason he phoned us was to get advice on how to apply his training to this specific situation. We told him how—the method appears later in this chapter—and he used it. The next day here is what he reported back to us.

He visited the businessman's office. The secretary's usual dour look was replaced by a smile. "He is in," she said pleasantly. She got up and went to open the door to the private office. Just then, it was opened from the inside, by the businessman.

"Come in, come in," he said, "I was thinking about you."

When they were seated, he continued, "Your policy is priced right. The coverage is fine. Let's fill out the forms right now."

The insurance man pulled out the forms, asked the key questions, and in a few minutes the forms were completed and signed.

"Would you like to pay in installments?" asked the insurance man.

"No. I'll pay for it now." He wrote out a check in full.

Reporting this to us later, the insurance man said, "In less than ten minutes, I was driving home in my car, stunned, with a check in my pocket for $43,000."

Needless to say, this success triggered more use of subjective communications by the agent, and more successes.

He was a graduate. You are still a trainee. As you train, though, you too can experience success. You must crawl, before you walk, before you run. So your practice sessions will begin with simple creative uses of the imagination, and then get to the method used by the insurance man. Small successes come first. Large successes come later.

HARNESSING CREATIVE IMAGINATION

I would now like to go over the steps to practice the use of the imagination, in order that I might make some further observations to assist you with each. Here are the steps:

Step 1. On awakening, go to your Alpha level by counting backwards from 5 to 1, and turning your eyes slightly upward, about twenty degrees above the normal plane of sight.

Step 2. Visualize according to previous instructions, recalling scenes from memory and "seeing" them out and away from your body.

Step 3. Now imagine other scenes. Imagination uses new scenes, not yet experienced. Premiere a new "mental movie," something that has not happened yet, but that you would like to happen.

Step 4. Make some positive statements or affirmations. See some suggestions below.

Step 5. Count yourself up from 1 to 5, feeling wide awake, better than before.

PERFECTING THE STEPS

Let us look at these steps again. Step 1 still presumes that you are in the practicing stage. That means you do it on awakening. This restriction can be eased as you progress. You can go to your Alpha level after lunch or in the evening before retiring. These are the best two times during the day. After you are satisfied with the results, you are then free to pick any time of day—dealer's choice.

Step 2 in your current practicing asks that you begin with memory scenes. This is visualization. We ask that you start imagination practice sessions with visualization, so that you can identify one from the other. Visualization reinforces present or past conditions or events by giving energy to these remembered scenes. So select success scenes to remember, thus reinforcing that success now.

Step 3 creates a shift from remembered scenes to desired scenes that have not yet taken place. This is dynamic meditation in its most creative form. These imagined scenes program you and other people, too, if they are "in the picture."

Step 4's positive statements act as commands to your "computer." You behave according to these commands. To make this a better day for you at the plant or office, create appropriate ones that apply. Here are some suggested statements:

- I remain energetic and enthusiastic all day.

- I am more and more patient, understanding, and compassionate of others.

- I have abundant creative ideas.

- I maintain my calm and wisdom in all situations.

- I maintain a healthy body and mind.

If you try to remember too much to do at the Alpha level, you drift up to Beta. So, adopt one or two statements to begin with. Later you can add to them or change them.

Step 5 is often slurred over by graduates and then they wonder why they still feel sleepy later. There are three times that the statement or command is given to be wide awake, feeling better than before, before you start the count up, when you reach the count of 3, and when you open your eyes at the count of 5. Make the statement all three times.

AN IMPORTANT CORRECTION

Another area where graduates often miss is in Step 2, visualizing "out and away from your body." If you are making the common mistake of visualizing on the inside of your eyelids, you are really using biological vision. This brings you up to twenty cycles where biological vision takes place. You do not want to be at Beta. You want to be at Alpha, ten cycles, where clairvoyance takes place.

Here is an exercise to correct this.

- Practice with your eyes open in a sitting position. Look straight ahead in a staring or gazing manner with your eyes not focused directly on anything in particular. By looking in this unfocused manner, the pupils tend to dilate.
- Now turn the eyes slightly upward, still open and still unfocused, at an angle of about twenty degrees above the horizontal, thus producing more Alpha, and helping you to hold on to that dimension.
- Now turn your eyes to the left, as far as they will go without forcing them. They are still open. They are still gazing in an unfocused way. They are still turned slightly upward. Now practice visualization in this position, remembering people, places or things that you have seen in the past, and describing them mentally to yourself in full detail and color.

This visualizing, with eyes open but not focused, disconnects the biological eyes from the visualizing process and so corrects the error of visualizing with the eyes. By looking to the left to do this, you involve the right brain more. You become more aware of an inner way of perceiving.

This develops a new feeling, with practice; a feeling of visualizing away from your body. This is an important feeling. Be aware of it. By recalling this feeling later, when you use visualization or imagination, you will automatically function with your intuitive right brain, at Alpha.

Once you have practiced visualization with your eyes open and in this position, begin practicing the use of the imagination. Switch from one to the other.

USING IMAGINATION FOR CLAIRVOYANCE NOW

When you switched from remembering past events and picturing them to creating new events and picturing them, you changed from visualization to imagination. Now you are going to use imagination in a way that will enhance clairvoyance.

Here is how:

Go to your Alpha level in the usual way. Now select a person whose name you have heard in your business but whom you have not yet seen. Describe that person to yourself. Do the best you know how. Say whatever comes to your mind—the color of hair, how tall, fat or thin—anything that pops into your thoughts as you imagine you see this person.

This method of practicing imagination leads to clairvoyance. You can use your neighbor's pets, if you have not seen them, or you can imagine a co-worker's house, one you have never seen.

In describing things you have never seen, you are enlisting the use of imagination. Instead of your making pictures with memory, you are making pictures with imagination.

When you mentally ask the question, "What does that person look like?" or "What does that house look like?" you are triggering more of the mind to go to work for you—the right hemisphere.

You are developing a feeling of clairvoyance. Later, by recalling that feeling, you will be at the right level to use your imagination for clairvoyance again.

Accuracy comes with practice. Do not be concerned about initial results. You will get curious results. Be patient as you practice, then later you can check on your accuracy by checking your mental picture against the actual person or house.

You will develop a feeling of an ideal level of thinking for clairvoyance. By remembering when you were accurate and how you felt being accurate, you will attain that ideal level for accurate clairvoyance again.

Once you are beginning to sense that feeling, you can then practice this method in your office.

If you have an appointment with somebody you have never seen, such as a salesman or job applicant, go to your Alpha level beforehand. Imagine what the person looks like. When the person arrives, note your "hits."

You will find that as you practice this, you will get better and better. Initial accuracy averages twenty-five percent. With practice, this increases to fifty percent. Eventually, you can attain a percentage of accuracy that exceeds eighty percent.

Some time after the person has left, use the occasion to practice visualization.

Go to your Alpha level and recall the person. Hat? Eyeglasses? Facial hair? Shape of nose, mouth, ears, eyebrows. Color of hair, eyes, skin. Body size. Color of suit, tie, shirt, belt, shoes, possibly socks.

By so doing you will be enhancing your visualization factor. As you improve your visualization factor, you will also be improving your imagination factor. Be sure to keep the person in mind as you recall details for both visualization and imagination.

We have not yet reached the point where we can use imagination for practical clairvoyant benefits. But we are at the doorstep.

"DISTANT VIEWING"

For several years, a project entitled "Distant Viewing" was conducted by SRI in California. Dr. Harold Puthoff and his colleagues asked volunteers to participate in the following way. After they were made comfortable in homey surroundings at the Institute, each volunteer was given a pad and pen and asked to sketch where a co-worker in New York was at the moment. Caught by surprise, but wanting to fulfill their obligations, the volunteers sketched whatever came to mind. Each sketch was dated and the time marked on it.

Meanwhile, the co-worker in New York was taking Polaroid pictures of where he was standing. These pictures were also marked with time and date. The pictures and sketches were then submitted to a committee, the members of which were selected for their objectivity—a lack of bias for or against the project. The committee then established whether each sketch was a "hit" or "miss."

Would you care to guess the percentage of sketches that contained "hits?" I am sure that your guess today is higher than your guess would have been before you started reading this book and practicing. There are two reasons for this: Your belief system has been somewhat altered; and your "guessing" ability has improved to the extent you have practiced up to this point. At any rate, the SRI success factor is eighty percent.

This does not mean that volunteers were eighty percent accurate, but that eighty percent of the volunteers had some accuracy.

Everybody has a right brain hemisphere.

USING ALPHA FOR A SUCCESSFUL MEETING

To make today a better day for you, your work at the Alpha level can now include more than goal-reaching programming; more than energy and enthusiasm affirmations; and more than efficient productivity pictures. You can now begin making this a better day by programming for specific encounters with certain persons to come off successfully. Here is how the clairvoyant executive can prepare for a meeting with an important person for a substantial transaction.

When you have practiced all of the exercises which you have been given so far, including using your imagination to describe a person or place you have not yet seen but are about to see, you are then ready to go to your level in a new way for an important matter.

1. Instead of counting from 5 to 1, count from 3 to 1, then count again from 10 to 1 to indicate you are about to work on a matter of special importance. Do this at night

before going to sleep. (This is what we referred to in an earlier chapter as the 3-to-1, 10-to-1 method.)

2. Select a person of the same sex as you who you know has done well in such transactions, similar to the one facing you on the following day. This person can be dead or alive. Visualize this expert by your side. If you do not know this expert, imagine him or her by your side.

3. Then program yourself—that is, say to yourself mentally —that you will awaken during the night or in the early morning, automatically, when the important person you are to meet the next day (identify that person by name) is at his or her ideal level to mentally discuss the project.

4. When you wake up automatically during the night or early morning, go to your level again by the 3-to-1, 10-to-1 procedure.

5. Visualize or imagine the expert you have selected. He or she will act as a consultant. See that expert by your side.

6. Next, visualize or imagine (depending on whether you are acquainted or not) the important person you are to deal with, and use the three-scene procedure.

   A. First scene: The important person is directly in front of you. You are greeting and welcoming that person.

   B. Second scene: Shift your awareness slightly to your left. Now talk mentally with the important person. Present your concepts and your ideas, your reasons for meeting with the person, just as you might be talking with this person in your office later. You should consult with the expert by your side, if you are in doubt as to what points to cover. Ask, and ideas will come to you. Present these to the important person mentally. See the important person reacting favorably and positively to your presentation. He or she is receptive and understands the points you are covering, and accepts the proposal.

   C. Third scene: Shift your awareness further to your

left. Now imagine the desired transaction completed and the end results already taking place, as though the meeting is in the past.

7. Do not count yourself up feeling wide awake. Instead, permit yourself to fall asleep from your Alpha level.

8. The next day, either in your morning practice or at the office, go through the same procedure again.

9. When the important person arrives, imagine that the expert is sitting at your side. Should a question arise that gives you pause, use the pause to mentally ask the expert.

WHY IT WORKS

Let us go over these steps again to better understand the purpose of each, and to provide additional details that contribute to effectiveness.

1. The 5-to-1 method for going to your Alpha level should be retained for routine programming. The 3-to-1, 10-to-1 method should be used for special projects of importance.

2. The right hemisphere is our connection to the nonphysical, spiritual, or causal plane. This is the realm of Higher Intelligence. The "expert" is symbolic of this greater intelligence to which we have access. By utilizing such a concept, insight, intuition, clairvoyance is reinforced.

3. The important person may be a late TV watcher or a drinker. He is more closed to subjective communication then. If he is asleep, there are times during sleep when his mind is more open to your mental message. Your mind will detect this and awaken you when so instructed.

4. Again, this is a special project of importance. Use the special countdown.

5. The expert replies to your questions as to what points might be made under 6B. The points need to be carefully

weighed because they must be mutually advantageous in nature. A transaction that benefits you and your company, but causes a problem for the other person's company, cannot be programmed to take place. The transaction must be of advantage to both parties. Your expert can be of help in this regard. Only that which is fair and correct will work.

6. Moving the scene from right to left has been found by years of research to add effectiveness. No hard scientific explanation is available, but we do have a few clues: Hypnotized subjects regressed to the past lean to the right; my children, in initial research, turned from right to left as they worked out a present problem and turned it into a forthcoming solution; the right brain controls the left side of the body. Keep in mind as you work on problems that the past situation or problem should be visualized to the right, the present changes straight ahead, and the future with no problem to the left.

7. There is no need to count yourself up unless you wish to be wide awake for Beta activities. Actually you wish to go in the opposite direction—to sleep at Theta and Delta.

8. Repetition prior to the meeting reinforces the night's programming.

9. During the meeting, the imagining of the expert present provides a "connection" to Higher Intelligence.

PRINCIPLES OF SUBJECTIVE COMMUNICATION

Perhaps you have been wondering just how close we are getting to religion when we enhance clairvoyance. Actually, the "no-man's-land" which traditionally separates science and religion is gradually being eroded.

As science gets to material frontiers within the atom, it has to use words that come close to describing a causal energy or intelligence. As religions modernize, they use words that come closer to science's concepts than to classical religion.

C. Thomas Sikking, who has taught leadership and motivational classes at Olympic College in Bremerton, Washington, conducts a seminar entitled "Creative Responsibility" which is also the title of a book he has written. Mr. Sikking has a broad background in business and law. He is also the senior minister at Portland Unity Church in Portland, Oregon. He is able to stand with one foot in the religious world and one foot in the material world quite comfortably. This is because "Creative Responsibility" does not get immersed in religion. It does assume, however, that there is a creative force (inner) behind the universe (outer) and that there is a meeting ground between our inner and outer realities.

The Silva Method brings us to this meeting ground. It thrives on unity, not separation. At the Alpha level, your imagination functions in superhuman ways because your right brain is your connection to a super intelligence. Break this connection and you are back to square one.

There are two easy ways to break the connection:

1. Do anything that moves you from Alpha to Beta.

2. Communicate anything that creates a separation.

So, the two main principles behind successful subjective communication are:

1. Communicate at Alpha.

2. Communicate as if you and the recipient were one.

REMOVING THE ILLUSION OF SEPARATION

Fact: You are part of an intelligence continuum that permeates the universe. Fact: If you feel "out of it," separated, you know who moved. You connect with this continuum when you use your imagination at the Alpha level. You connect even better with the correct frame of mind. The correct frame of mind is one of teamwork, with all mankind on the same team.

Our competitive society cultivates one-upmanship. There is

often a dog-eat-dog attitude in intracompany jealousies and in competition between companies. When using subjective communication, this attitude breaks off the connection. A more cooperative and compassionate attitude becomes more successful.

A sales manager is using subjective communication to encourage a more positive attitude on the part of a recently employed salesman. He is alone in his office. He has used the 3-to-1, 10-to-1 method to go to Alpha. If he says "You moron. One more bad week and I'll give you good reason to feel negative," the connection has been broken.

On the other hand, if he says mentally, "The world is what we make it. Be enthusiastic. Your sales will increase, and give you something to be enthusiastic about," the message will get through.

When using subjective communication, avoid polarity. Avoid statements that put down, that criticize, that set you or your company apart. Communicate *what* is right, rather than *who* is right. Distance does not matter. The message gets through. It gets through below the conscious level.

A typical subjective communication by the clairvoyant executive to a potential client or customer might express the following points:

– The advantages of the product or service

– The advantages of dealing with his firm

– His personal concern for the welfare of the client or customer

– Other short-term benefits

– Other long-term benefits

A typical subjective communication would also:

– Be truthful

– Be fair—inequality breaks the connection

– Be aboveboard—trickery boomerangs

– Be mutually respectful—foster a meeting of the minds

– Be creative—you are using the creative realm

The key is to overcome the illusion of separateness induced by salesman-customer and other such business polarities.

During the first few years of life, we use both left and right hemispheres equally. In those early years, we learn about twenty-five times more per day than in later years, when the left brain becomes more dominant. The old adage, "Be as a child" is now revealed by scientific research to have practical dollars and cents value.

OPPORTUNITIES FOR SUBJECTIVE COMMUNICATION

You have just begun a new phase of your own personal development. You have a key that unlocks the potential of your mind. You have graduated to a new level of effectiveness as you begin to employ inner powers that can shape the future, powers that work for you night and day.

You have begun to activate the right brain to work in harmony with your left brain. Your reason and logic are now supplemented with intuition and clairvoyance. Together they can reach out and create personal progress, business progress, world progress. You are programming for this progress with the Silva Method. Its applications in daily business life are as comprehensive as that business life is itself.

Let us first review three separate programming approaches that are available to you with the Silva Method as presented so far on these pages.

1. *Alpha affirmations*

2. *The Three Fingers Technique,* programmed initially at Alpha, but used mostly at Beta

3. *Important Event Programming* using expert, optimum time and the three-scene procedure at Alpha

Alpha affirmations can be made any time of the day or night to strengthen your resolve, well-being, energy, skill, understanding, motivation, optimism, enthusiasm, and even success with the Silva Method.

The applications of simple visualization and imagination

programming techniques at the Alpha level range from personal betterment on the job, to a more fulfilling and productive day for the company.

The Three Fingers Technique can be used to increase your intelligence whenever needed, reading technical papers or reports, attending meetings, ending indecision, being in the right place at the right time.

The Important Event Programming, for which the procedure has been spelled out in this chapter, can be used in advance of meetings where a critical decision on the part of another person will be made. Some examples might be:

1. Job interview

2. Major sales event

3. Labor-management matter

4. Court proceeding

5. Proposal presentation

6. Problem with subordinate

7. Problem with government representative

THE HUMAN MIND AT WORK

As we proceed in the chapters ahead, additional Silva Method Techniques will be provided, and we will delve deeper into their applications for specific situations. It will be impossible to cover all possible situations, but you will be able to adapt these applications more flexibly as you see multiple uses.

In the Silva Method training, we repeat the programming that the Alpha level can be used for benefits, "any benefit that you desire." And this is so.

The human mind at work in the world manipulates matter until it forms civilizations. Living patterns are modified and refined. Changes occur at the individual level and at the world level. The mind that resists change, ceases to have ideas of its own, ceases to think constructively. The mind that resonates with change, grows, expands, and survives in the evolving world.

8

Handling Difficult People and Solving Discipline Problems

The scene is the Hilton Hawaiian Village in Honolulu, 1972. My writing associate, Dr. Stone, has just given the opening address at a conference on clairvoyance and psychic functioning. The workshops are now under way.

One workshop leader has just explained her brain wave measuring equipment. Jean Millay, biofeedback researcher, will now let the audience view the rhythm of her brain waves on a standard movie screen—one of the first demonstrations of this equipment to a large audience.

"There will be static at first," she says. "But then, as I relax and go to my Alpha level, you will see a harmonic pattern."

The electrodes are attached to her head. She sits in a chair beneath the screen and the equipment is activated. The screen shows a confusion of light patterns. As Dr. Stone observes from the rear of the auditorium, the static persists, despite efforts to adjust it. Her assistant approaches him.

"She asks that you help her," he says. "I'm sorry," replies Dr. Stone. "Tell her I know nothing about that equipment." A moment later, the young assistant returns. "She says to come anyhow."

With that, Dr. Stone understands what is needed. As he walks down the aisle toward her, he visualizes her as serene and tranquil, and "sees" her responding to his supportive, peaceful, loving concern. Before he reaches her, the screen suddenly changes from the chaotic light patterns to a beautiful pattern of symmetry.

The scene is now 1981, on the mainland. Jean Millay is now addressing the convention of the American Educational Research Association. Instead of a standard movie screen, she is using a "light sculpture," a box with rows of lights in different colors, which, when activated by brain waves, gives a three-dimensional effect. Each color represents a different brain frequency. "With the appropriate focus of attention," she states, "the brain can produce powerful insights."

I relate these two incidents for two main reasons.

First, it gives us an idea of the excellent progress being made in a ten-year period in this field of research, using Dr. Millay as an example. In a way, it is satisfying to witness this research being investigated by educators. But at the same time, it is frustrating to see the slow rate at which findings are being applied at the classroom level. Business and industry are also "dragging their feet" in applying research findings.

Second, the Honolulu incident demonstrates the ability of one human mind to affect another—in a positive direction. And that is the thrust of this chapter.

ONE PERSON'S BRAIN WAVES AFFECT ANOTHER'S

At the Third World Psychotronic Conference, held in Monte Carlo in 1975, a researcher asked for two volunteers. Two women came down the aisle. He seated them facing each other. Each was hooked up to brain encephalograph (EEG) equipment. A large dial behind each chair, visible to the audience, showed the predominant brain level.

He asked the women to relax. In a few moments, they were both showing fourteen to fifteen cycles per second. "Now help each other to relax," he instructed them. Almost immediately, the dials showed a slowing down to eleven to twelve cycles.

Then the researcher turned to the audience. "Everybody now help them to relax," he said. Again, the two dials reflected a further slowing down to about ten cycles.

No instructions were given as to how to help the two volunteers to relax. Yet, without specific methodology, the two volunteers were able to help each other and the audience was able to help them.

This is because the very concept of relaxation is relaxing. This brain wave effect we have on each other is not lessened by distance. Maimonides Dream Laboratory experiments conducted under the supervision of Dr. Stanley Krippner years ago demonstrated this when volunteer married couples were used. The man and wife were placed in different hospitals about seven miles apart and each was hooked up to biofeedback and physiological monitoring devices.

"Your wife just died—no, she is fine. We are just testing."

When this statement was made, the instrumentation showed a sudden shock effect—heart, blood pressure, brain waves. And, seven miles away, the instrumentation monitoring the wife showed a similar effect at the very same instant.

Even greater distances were involved in Russian experiments with animals. The mother of a litter was taken out to sea in a submarine. When a member of the litter was killed on land, hundreds of miles away, the mother instantaneously reacted measurably.

As we become aware of our effect on each other, we become in control of that effect. As we realize that our brain waves circle the earth in length, we no longer consider the distance from home to office or office to warehouse as a factor.

THE MANAGER AS A BROADCASTER

You have a broadcasting station. Your head *is* that station. It is a one-man station. You are its engineer and its program director. Your audience is quite selective. You reach anybody you think of.

The station is a money maker. You can use it to handle difficult people, solve discipline problems, iron out personality conflicts, and dissolve individual nonproductivity.

If this is beginning to sound mouth-watering to you, so much so that you decide impatiently to use the method before practicing the countdown exercise for enhancing Alpha or the visualization and imagination exercises for clairvoyance, I am sorry to say, Mr. Executive, that you will become impatient waiting for results.

The weeks of daily practice of the Silva Method are necessary for controlled results. The natural abilities are latent within all of us, but so are the abilities to play tennis or to use a typewriter. Those abilities need to be exercised in a certain way in order to bring the desired results.

BROADCASTING HARMONY

George Otis, former general manager of the Lear Corporation, and now an evangelist who heads a nationally syndicated television series called "High Adventure," launched a radio and television station in a conclave of southern Lebanon surrounded by PLO terrorists, UN peacekeeping forces, Israeli troops, and Syrian forces. The station uses the Gospel and country music to broadcast harmony to warring Moslems, Christians and Jews. The station has been a force for peace. Said a senior military officer, "The station has been worth two divisions toward bringing peace to the region." Music is right brain "stuff."

"Doc" Severinsen, the colorful band leader on the Johnny Carson show, is in a sense a business manager. He uses the Silva Method. The success he attains as a business manager is reflected in the harmony his musicians are able to produce.

You, as a business manager, can be a factor for disorder or order, conflict or cooperation, discord or harmony, inefficiency or efficiency, a team that is pulling apart or a team that is pulling together. With the Silva Method, you are able to induce teamwork.

In this chapter, we are going to treat specific situations with which you might be faced. All situations involving human problems can be solved when *all* of the brain is used—all of the manager's brain, but also all of the brain of the other person involved.

A fish uses all of its brain, naturally. It is common knowledge that salmon always return to their home waters for breeding, even if this means miles of travel and arduous upstream journeys. After the Mount St. Helens eruption, biologists expected the salmon, some weighing over twenty-five pounds, to die trying to head up the Cowlitz and Toutle rivers as they usually do, for now these two rivers were completely clogged with mud and debris. To their surprise, the salmon avoided these rivers and instead headed up the nearby Kalama River, which was free of debris and mud. How did the salmon know?

When all of the brain is working, instinct and intuition come through—all of the brain for all of the fish.

It would be ideal for all of the workers in a company to activate all of their brains. With the Silva Method, such unanimity of brain functioning would work miracles for the company (and is already doing so for many companies) as well as for the manager.

In Venezuela, there is a governmental effort to upgrade the intelligence level of the whole population. This unique project is being conducted through the efforts of the Venezuela Ministry for the Development of Intelligence, working not only with existing educational institutions but also with the mass media. The goal is to establish an "internal creativity."

You are a good beginning in your firm. If you were to look upon your own development, as a clairvoyant and as a subjective communicator, as a means to get a jump on others, you could be separating yourself from the other salmon and swimming up an unclogged stream—alone.

As you discover your own broadcasting ability, broadcast the existence of such an ability to others. Then as they trigger theirs, they become even better receivers of yours. The result: an unbeatable team.

SUBJECTIVE COMMUNICATION SIMPLICITY

The following is a catalogue description of a university course entitled "Communications for Managers":

This course gives you an understanding of one-to-one communications, communication in organizations, and mass media communications—all from the standpoint of the manager. You will learn what works best, what goes wrong, and how to help others communicate more effectively.

Can you imagine the vast amount of detail covered by this course? It covers enhancing oral communications which can bog down in approach, personality, vocabulary, tone, and contents. It also covers memo writing, letter writing, and report writing, and you know how many do's and don'ts can be involved to get the message across through the written word. It has to cover the press release, advertising copy, bulletins, newsletters, and feature stories for newspapers and magazines as part of publicity activities in mass communications. Formidable detail.

Let us write a catalogue description of another course entitled "Subjective Communications for Managers":

> This course gives you training in communicating at the Alpha level through visualization and imagination.

What does this course cover? Relaxation, visualization, and imagination in a statesmanlike way; period.

The university course is a left brain course. It goes into objective communication in all its detail. The left brain eats up detail. In left brain approaches, detail tends to proliferate. The course I just described is a right brain course. The right brain does not get into detail. It sees the bird's-eye view, the whole picture. The whole picture is a picture of wholeness—a unity behind the universe.

Subjective communication is simple. It rests on one firm principle: The truth, compassionately sent. This is going to be an easy chapter for you.

CASE STUDIES—HOW TO USE THEM

Here are three common managerial situations. Using the methods we have already provided, as summarized at the end of the last chapter, how would you use the Silva Method to solve the problems they pose?

To make this an optimum learning experience, so that you are better able to apply the Silva Method to your own managerial situations, it is recommended that you read a case and then decide how you would go about handling it, before reading the answers supplied. In this way, you will be practicing such a determination, so that when the time comes for you to use the Silva Method, you will be better able to answer for yourself the question "How?"

This is not to suggest that there is only one Silva Method application that will work. Any way that entails the use of the right brain, of triggering techniques, of subjective communication will help because it is using more of your brain. The answers supplied will be those that seem most appropriate. Alternatives will also be noted.

THE OVERLENIENT FOREMAN

Case Study I. Nathan J. has recently been made foreman to replace a man who left for a better job. Nat, as he is known to his fellow workers, has always been well-liked, conscientious, and loyal to the company. But now, as foreman, he is much too permissive. He does not enforce the rules. Productivity is slipping. Discipline is poor. You have had three meetings with Nat. During the first, you called Nat's attention to the shift in attitude that the foreman's job required and how less socializing and more supervising was required. He agreed. During the second, you cited specific instances of rule infractions and how they endangered worker safety. He agreed. During the third, you "socked it to him." Discipline had to shape up. Production had to increase. He agreed. Now you realize that Nat's eager-to-agree attitude is a cover-up for his unwillingness to discuss the matter and probably his unwillingness to change. He is a good man. Demotion could be demoralizing to him and to others. Also, having recommended Nat as foreman, you could erode your own position with your supervisor. What do you do? How do you use the Silva Method to solve this problem?

DELICATE RULES NEGOTIATIONS

Case Study II. A quality control person has been discharged for overlooking defects that could have disastrous results for consumers of a processed food. The administration has backed you up both in your decision and during the subsequent grievance proceedings instituted by the union that wanted the man reinstated.

At first, negotiations centered around whether the discharged inspector had willfully overlooked the defects, and, if so, whether it was to pacify management's preference not to "rock the boat," or whether it was the inspector's own disinclination to take an antagonistic posture toward his fellow workers by disclosing the defects.

Now, these negotiations are involving government agency representatives who ordered the product pulled from the shelves. They are now reviewing the company's quality control procedures, especially inspectors' attitudes and possible laxness or permissiveness. This has had a polarizing effect and has developed into a "Catch-22" situation: You are damned if you did (rehire)—by the government; and damned if you didn't—by the union.

After a particularly frustrating three-hour afternoon session, a final meeting is scheduled for nine o'clock the next morning. Can you use the Silva Method to solve this problem? If so, how?

THE SECRET DRINKER

Case Study III. Ralph P. was a veteran salesman of your company's printing services. It was often necessary for him to take an existing or potential customer out to lunch to discuss business. These were invariably two- or three-martini lunches. Since Ralph's success as a salesman over the years was appreciated, the alcoholic lunches were not only condoned, but paid for by the company. You had OK'd the expense vouchers.

For the past six months, Ralph's sales were slipping, while younger salesmen with less experience and fewer connections in the trade were moving ahead. At morning meetings with Ralph, you smelled liquor on his breath. Reluctantly, you checked his desk. A bottle of liquor was found in a drawer and a flask in his coat pocket. When confronted with this, Ralph made light of the situation. The moment of decision has arrived. Do you discharge this veteran? You cannot force him to stop drinking or seek help. Can the Silva Method help? If so, how?

APPLYING THE SILVA METHOD IN CASE I

Suggested Technique. Nathan J. is insecure as a foreman. He has accepted the new title and new pay but not the new responsibilities. Whether he is insecure about giving the correct orders, or insecure about having them complied with matters little. This basic insecurity has caused him to turn a deaf ear to advice and criticism. Objective communication is blocked. Subjective communication is indicated. The procedure is to go to the Alpha level with the 5-to-1 method and visualize Nathan. Re-create the first meeting and see it off to your right. Go through the same points as before, explaining in an understanding, noncritical way how less socializing and more supervision would benefit the company and everybody concerned. Re-create the second meeting, moving the picture a bit closer to straight ahead but still slightly to the right as it is still in the past. Again, go over the rule infractions and review why the rules were established, pointing out the safety risks posed by those infractions. Re-create the third meeting, moving the picture still closer to straight ahead. In a statesmanlike, diplomatic manner discuss the benefits to all of his increased attention to discipline and productivity. The next scene is in the future, so imagine it to the left. In your imagination, see Nathan accepting his responsibilities. See him supervising with confidence and skill. See him as a conscientious and effective foreman.

Alternate Techniques. If you consider this a critical problem, you can program to awake at night at the best time to communicate subjectively, and you can create an expert psychologist to assist you. If you consider this a minor situation, you can have additional objective talks with Nathan, putting your three fingers together to say the right thing at the right time to get through to Nathan.

APPLYING THE SILVA METHOD IN CASE II

Suggested Technique. This is an important meeting. The importance can be considered by management to be saving face—not letting the union get away with anything. The importance for the union, on the other hand, can also be saving face—showing its members that it does not let management get away with anything. The solution here lies in avoiding the polarity battlefront and in not addressing *who* is right but *what* is right. The party that needs to win is the consumer. From the consumer's point of view, it does not matter whether the union or management wins or whether or not the inspector gets rehired. What matters is that the inspector not have a job with the same critical inspection responsibility. This will satisfy the government agency, too. Tonight's Silva Method Alpha work then is to use the full "important event" method with the key figures in the picture. These are the union negotiators and the management negotiators. Before going to sleep, go to the Alpha level with your 3-to-1, 10-to-1 method. At Alpha, select an expert in labor management relations to be by your side. Program yourself to awaken at the optimum time to communicate with the labor and company people, identify them by visualizing each in turn. Permit yourself to fall asleep. When you awaken, again go to the Alpha level with the same double count. Welcome your expert by your side. See the labor and company people arriving in the meeting room. The scene is straight ahead. They are cordial and shaking hands. The second scene is slightly to your left. Offer your "what is right" solution. See all agreeing. See the details being discussed amiably. The third and final scene is the inspector at work happily in a less critical area of quality control. Your colleagues are content. Labor union representatives are satisfied. End your session. You should repeat this in the morning, either before you leave the house or in the office.

Alternate Technique. If your analysis is different, you might want to program for the inspector to be hired by another firm. If this solves the problem, and does not cause a problem for either the inspector or his new firm, this could be a viable solution and one that would work with the Silva Method, but would have to be initiated prior to the vital meeting. For several nights, program through imaged pictures, seen progressively to the left, that this hiring will take place. See the interviews. See the hiring handshake. If you keep the hiring company unidentifiable in your pictures, you will avoid creating a problem block.

APPLYING THE SILVA METHOD IN CASE III

Suggested Technique. Ralph is a victim of his own fears. Perhaps it is the fear of retiring, or being retired, or the fear of failing, or the fear of dying, or the fear of aging. Whatever the fear, Ralph has turned to the faithful crutch he has leaned on during sales lunches—alcohol. Because of the absence of Ralph's desire to seek help or to help himself, the Silva Method of subjective communication should be used to get that point over to him on a survival level. Brain neurons are programmed for survival. He has been programming his neurons for his own demise. He needs to reverse the process. Go to your Alpha level. See Ralph in a scene straight ahead. Talk to him on a spirits to spiritual basis. Liquor is killing him. He is here to create. Call on him to live for the Creator's sake. He has a disease—alcoholism—and needs to seek outside help. See Ralph joining an organization such as Alcoholics Anonymous and ultimately tossing out the bottle and emptying the flask down the sink. Move the scene further to the left. See Ralph back as his old self—a veteran salesman, drinking mineral water at lunch.

Alternate Techniques. Other methods of handling this problem will evolve in the pages ahead, but with Silva Method approaches already covered, alternate techniques would be in the lines of subjective conversation. You might prefer to begin with a straight-on conversation: "Wouldn't it be better for all concerned if you stopped drinking?" or "Cut down, Ralph, you'll sell better. Maybe you should get help with this problem."

IS SUBJECTIVE COMMUNICATION WEIRD?

When you use the Silva Method of subjective communication and you see the lax foreman tighten up and use his authority; when you see union and management reach a harmonious compromise; when you see the alcoholic salesman going to a clinic; you might at first think it coincidence. After more successes, you begin to realize that "it works."

The acceptance that it works still does not erase the feeling that it is weird or "far out." Our lifelong left brain orientation demands a logical explanation.

The world of science has been forced to address itself to obtaining this logical explanation. Considerable progress is being made. The incentive appears to be coming from two directions:

1. The U.S. Defense Department has allowed the expenditure of funds for the study of psychic phenomena and how they can be used in military strategies.

2. The Soviet Union has been pursuing the study of psychic phenomena for many years and is considered to be more advanced than we are in this field.

As science responds, more and more "far out" abilities of the mind are being examined in the laboratory. Psychic ability is becoming more and more openly used by police departments, geologists, and archeologists. More and more businesses dare to utilize so-called extrasensory perception (ESP).

The business manager who is able to influence events outside of himself by his own direct behavior is exercising psychokinesis. Psychokinesis is being studied in the laboratories of a number of prestigious scientific organizations. However, it may take years before a rational, logical, reasonable left brain explanation is reached.

What do we do in the meantime? How do we live with something we do not understand? A building contractor on the East Coast was having precognitive dreams. He dreamt about accidents and fires before they happened. He argued with family members to change their plans but they laughed at his reasons. One of his predictions made the wire services and then came true. He did not understand his ability. He developed all the symptoms of a nervous breakdown and had to retire from his business activity prematurely. This was thirty years ago. He could not talk about his ability as readily as we can today.

Today, psychic ability is no longer a taboo subject. It has come of age.

CIRCUMVENTING LEFT BRAIN RATIONALE

Why do we cry? Why do we dream? Why do color schemes affect the way we think or feel? Why does soft music affect our mood? These are right brain phenomena for which we have no logical left brain explanation. There are other right brain phenomena. We have grown to accept them. They are no longer considered to be phenomena. We have circumvented the left brain's requirement for logical reasons.

Despite the fact that our left brained society prides itself in its pragmatism and rationalism, it accepts many things about the human mind and nature that it cannot comprehend. The tremendous powers of the human mind are becoming accepted even though they are beyond the powers of the human mind to comprehend.

"Wait a minute," you say, "Does not the brain have the power to comprehend its own powers?" This is a good point. Let me put it this way: Half the brain does not have the power to comprehend the powers of the full brain. Does that sit better logically?

Once we activate the right brain, as you are now doing, it is the whole brain that then addresses itself to its own understanding; and that understanding becomes possible.

Researchers at Caltech in California have found that the right hemisphere is far more aware and sophisticated than has been previously assumed, and that it communicates what it knows to the left brain, apparently through the common brain stem.

As you use subjective communication in your business, and cause "miracles" to occur between difficult people, in discipline situations, in behavioral problems, you begin to accept these "miracles" as just the manifestation of another one of your managerial skills.

Others will begin to admire you. When they question you, you can always point to this book and the Silva Method training you gave yourself. The "far out" then becomes the "in" thing.

SETTING A LEFT BRAIN, RIGHT BRAIN EXAMPLE

John R., a Silva Method graduate, is a successful Realtor. He has a number of licensed agents working for him. John believes that the best way a manager can maintain a high level of productivity and good discipline is to be a productive, disciplined person himself. So, he keeps a high level of motivation by maintaining a successful sales record. Here is how John applies the Silva Method to make a specific sale.

He uses the 3-to-1, 10-to-1 method to enter his Alpha level just before falling asleep. He then imagines an expert by his side. This person could have lived in the past or could be alive now. This person could be male or female. John R. then programs himself (gives himself instructions) to wake up at the proper time when his potential customer of the next day will be at the optimum state to accept his subjective communication. He then goes to sleep.

In describing his approach to me, the graduate explained, "With a high-priced piece of land or large building, I go 'all out' with the Silva Method." So we will assume, in describing his method to you now, that this is an important, high-priced piece of property.

I awake at some time during the night and I immediately use the 3-to-1, 10-to-1 method to go to Alpha. I greet my expert and imagine the potential customer. I then move the scene slightly to the left and explain the advantages of the property. I ask my expert if I have left anything out. Often, ideas come to me that seem unimportant to me, but are obviously important to the potential customer. Again, I move the scene to the left and see the customer, appreciating the information and considering the purchase.

Using this method, he does not create a possible problem by programming for the actual sale to be made to this particular customer. By avoiding seeing the sale clinched, he keeps the problem-creating block from entering the picture and is able to get his subjective sales pitch concluded effectively. The result is a high level of sales.

The free will of the customer must be respected. Free will is a universal gift to all people. We cannot program successfully *against* free will. But we can program successfully *for* mutual benefits. Our graduate is going as far as he can with a specific person. He could have chosen to program for the actual sale instead, by not identifying the customer.

We have left out one ingredient which we will cover in the next chapter. This real estate executive uses the Silva Method to determine the best media in which to advertise the property, the best page of a newspaper, and even the best day, thus saving time and money.

THE OBJECTIVE, SUBJECTIVE MANAGER

You are a good example to your staff, but perhaps only a good *objective* example. A manager is a manager because he has shown himself to have a broad spectrum of knowledge about the business, certainly broader than one single job skill. As a manager, you are looked up to for that reason. Your people are impressed by your actions and your words. These are objective. These are only half the story.

How do you impress your staff? Objectively, you do what you have been doing—do your job well and do everybody else's job well. Subjectively, you go to your Alpha level and "see" those jobs being done well.

Information is impressed on brain cells when the brain is functioning at its energetic and synchronized best. That has been found to be the Alpha level, the optimum brain frequency for impressing information on ourselves and on others.

When the business manager has his mind under control, and when he uses that control to go to the Alpha level and program, he is more effective. When he uses Alpha programming to "see" activities taking place efficiently and creatively, he is setting a subjective example for others. His brain neurons are resonating with those of others involved in the activities, and they are being programmed, too. By getting their brain neurons to resonate with his in a common goal, he is encouraging teamwork.

WAYS TO PROGRAM PEOPLE

We all have free will. We cannot take free will away from others with our own will. That would be creating a problem for other people. Brain neurons are programmed for solving problems, not creating them.

The business manager can go to his Alpha level and see his ten employees all working in harmony, with no individual irritations arising to spoil the teamwork. This will usually produce the desired effects unless there is some kind of "blocking problem," as explained below.

Let's assume, first, that there are no such problems; that solutions to the manager's working day can take effect without interfering with the free will of others. Here, then, is how you go about using your Alpha level of mind to program for better discipline, more harmonious employee relations, and "a good day."

- Use the 5-to-1 method when you awake in the morning. Turn your eyes slightly upward and visualize your office, shop, store, or plant. Recall a time when you were delighted with discipline, and visualize it to your right. If you can't recall such a time, imagine what it would look like.

- Now visualize the same condition with tomorrow's setup, moving the picture slightly to your left. Turn your head to the right again and visualize a time when there was no friction or discord; or imagine what it would look like.

- Again, translate that picture into tomorrow's conditions and see it to your left. Repeat this process for any other factors you wish to program for, such as improved efficiency, volume, quality, etc. End by making some positive affirmations about yourself; then, count yourself up 1 to 5 feeling better than before.

Suppose, however, there is a "blocking problem." An example might be if one of your employees is a chain smoker and is working closely with another employee who is a nonsmoker. Because they each have free will, your visualization of these two working together harmoniously will have no effect on their daily battle:

"Put it out." "I just lit it."

You can handle this as a separate problem. The approach to smoking and drinking problems has been discussed earlier. Unless you deal with it, it will continue to inject disharmony into your visualization. Nevertheless, creative visualization is a powerful tool.

EVERYTHING WORKS BETTER

Richard Bach, Mind Control graduate and author of one of the "hottest" books ever written, *Jonathan Livingston Seagull,* explains: "Creative visualization is really what's behind the Silva Method; that is, whatever you can visualize, you can actualize."

That is putting it squarely on the line. It is putting teeth into the old saw, "What man can conceive, he can achieve." If you can conceive of "a good day," . . . Need I finish the sentence?

Everything works better when *you* work; but objective work, as productive as it is, is not the only work you must do. You must also do subjective work, using ten cycles per second to resonate with other minds and to get everything to work still better.

How a million-dollar insurance salesman in Pawtucket, Rhode Island used the Silva Method was related in the Pawtucket *Times.* He and three others in his office took the Silva Method training and all but one decided to put it through a test period. During that period the three increased production for the whole staff by 490 percent.

Said a reporter for another newspaper, "The amazing,

almost scary thing is, it works. Students are trained to be 'functioning psychics' who can turn their ESP on or off at will. Students learn all this (and more) by learning the function in a natural state of mind—the Alpha level."

Everything works better. In this chapter, we have addressed discipline and other personnel problems, but we have used only a few examples. To help you see the wide range of applications even within this narrow scope, here are some additional problem situations and typical solution pictures that can help.

Ten Problem Situations and How to Handle Them Subjectively

Problem Situation	Solution Picture
Your assistant feels he does not receive enough recognition.	Praise him subjectively. Hold an imaginary testimonial dinner in his honor.
A long-time employee resents a new man just hired.	Remind him subjectively that the new man could be his son. See the two working harmoniously together.
A technician objects to too much paper work.	See time going faster for him while he is doing it.
A complaining employee keeps talking about his previous company.	Have a subjective conversation about the pluses and minuses in any job. See him making the best of the pluses.
An employee feels there are salary inequities.	Appeal subjectively to his tolerance of temporary injustice, assuring him that "this too shall pass."
Two men never get along with each other.	Forgive each one in turn and ask their forgiveness of each other. See it happening.

Problem Situation	Solution Picture
An employee does not like the work assigned to him.	See him unhappy. Move the picture to the left, as you encourage him. See him better adjusted.
An employee is absent frequently because of poor physical condition.	A future chapter will cover this more directly, but meanwhile hold pictures of him in radiant good health.
An employee continuously discusses his home problems at work.	In a subjective conversation, encourage him to stuff his problems in a sack at his front door when he leaves for work. See him doing it.
An employee's wife is making him dissatisfied with his job.	Have a three-way subjective conversation directed at the benefits of positive attitudes.

ZEROING IN ON STUBBORN SITUATIONS

When a clairvoyant manager is faced with a difficult person who does not respond to objective approaches, the subjective approach is needed. This subjective approach frequently needs to be focused specifically on that person rather than on the team. Here is one effective method:

- Program yourself at Alpha level before going to sleep, that you will wake up automatically at the optimum time to program the problem person.
- When you awaken, again go to your level and visualize the problem person directly in front of you.
- Mentally talk to him about the need to abide by the rules, get along with others, or whatever else contributes to the problem. (More steps to follow.)

It is as though you are talking to the "fundamental" person, the inner nature of the person that is more intelligent and understanding. It is as though the problem person is under hypnosis, and you are bypassing that person's critical consciousness. When you explain what is wrong about this person's behavior and set forth the changes that need to be made, you are programming a change for the better in that person. Do not risk "breaking the connection" by resorting to recrimination. Instead, make it a heart-to-heart talk, emphasizing the mutual benefits to all concerned, and how you wish to help him to harmonize more with the others and to synchronize their efforts for greater productivity, ease and enjoyment.

A Word That Commands Correction

- Now, select a phrase or word that you can speak normally in the work environment—like "It helps" or "It is better." Mentally tell the problem person that whenever you speak that word or phrase objectively on the job he will instantly understand the need for corrected behavior. The word or phrase will not be used out of context but will occur in the normal course of conversation. "Whenever you hear '(word or phrase)' you will automatically understand that you are wrong and must change and cooperate."

- Move the scene slightly to the left. It is the office or shop. You say the word or phrase. See the problem person understanding and willing to cooperate.

- Move the scene again slightly to the left. See the problem person no longer a problem. See him happy. See everybody happy.

- End your session by permitting yourself to fall asleep.

You can use the word or phrase on the job the very next day and see the results. The undisciplined person becomes more disciplined. The problem person becomes less of a problem. Subjective communication has taken place.

And this is so.

9
Managing Time More Efficiently with the Silva Method

When the business executive studies techniques to manage his time more effectively, he finds himself assessing priorities, sequences, and schedules. He is encouraged to delegate more authority and to extricate himself from nonessentials. This is all commendable; but it is only the beginning.

With the Silva Method, the business executive finds that clairvoyance saves lengthy testing, in going through time-consuming steps to find the right way. His mind already knows the best way. All he has to do is ask it.

The Baltimore *Sun* recently reported how a yellow crayoned circle on a map of Egypt, supplied to a California research team by a psychic, resulted in the discovery of remains reported to be the palaces of Anthony and Cleopatra. Stephen Schwartz, former research assistant with the Department of the Navy, was quoted as saying, "We are not trying to prove that psychic capacity exists in people. We are saying flatly that this represents a tool that is not used as much as it should be to make all kinds of discoveries."

In this chapter, we will cover ways to manage time more efficiently—not only the hours of the day, but also the days of the week and the weeks of the year—by discovering the right route to take clairvoyantly.

Let us begin by reminding you of the Realtor who used the Silva Method to sell an important piece of property, as described in the previous chapter.

ASKING YOUR MIND FOR ANSWERS

The Realtor who had an expensive property to sell, which promised a substantial commission, would use the "important situation" procedure to plan the selling strategy.

This selling strategy might entail a direct mail solicitation, a telephone campaign, an advertising schedule or any combination of these. With the Silva Method, the best approach—the one through which the property might eventually be sold—can be determined in advance with sizable savings in time and money.

This Realtor used the Silva Method to determine the best communication channel. It turned out to be advertising. He then determined the best medium—television, radio, or newspaper. The Silva Method answer: newspaper. He then determined which was the right newspaper, what section in that newspaper would be most effective, and even what day of the week to advertise!

The results were so successful that it became his standard procedure whenever a sizeable property listing was obtained.

CLAIRVOYANT CHOICE
DETERMINATION

Here is the method as applied to the particular real estate project:

- Use the 3-to-1, 10-to-1 method before going to sleep to enter the Alpha level.
- Invite an imaginary consultant to appear in the picture as you visualize the property to be sold.
- Instruct yourself to awaken at the appropriate time to work on this project. Fall asleep from Alpha level.
- When you awaken during the night, again use the 3-to-1, 10-to-1 method to go to Alpha.
- Welcome your imaginary consultant. Again, visualize the property. Then ask the first question that needs to be decided. In this case, that question was, "Do I

contact the buyer by telephone, mail, radio, television, or newspapers?"

- Then use the elimination method by pairing two choices and getting an answer. How that answer comes is explained below. In this example, four communication methods need to be eliminated to yield the one that should be used.

- Assuming that newspaper is the one indicated, use the elimination method to select the particular newspaper.

- Use the elimination method to select the proper section of that newspaper.

- Use the elimination method to pinpoint the best day to advertise.

- Thank your imaginary consultant, and end your session by permitting yourself to fall asleep.

Here is what we mean by the elimination method. Pick two alternatives, say, correspondence or telephone. Ask the question "Which should I use—correspondence or telephone?" Then permit your mind to wander and think of something else. In a few moments, come back to the project and again mentally ask that question. An answer will come. It will pop into your mind—telephone. Now do the same to compare telephone with the next medium. Another medium will be eliminated. Continue until only one medium results. That is the one your supermind is telling you to use.

Some clairvoyant practitioners prefer to use an imaginary television set. They turn on the imaginary television set to where only static or "snow" is seen. They ask the question "Which should I use—correspondence or telephone?" Then they switch to an operating channel and they see the answer on the imaginary television screen.

CLAIRVOYANT DETERMINATIONS— POSSIBLE SCOPE

You are at your desk. You are faced with a job that needs to be done within a certain time limit. There are a number of ways you can get the job done in time. If there was only one way to get the job done, there would be no time factor problem. You would go about the only available route in the most efficient way. However, as you sit there, you see two or more ways to get that job done. Which one do you use?

Your competency as a manager may be on the line. Your judgment is being tested. It is not the first time for such a test. You have been right more often than wrong in the past. That is probably why you are a business manager.

If you want to make your decision in the same way you have decided before, fine, that is your choice. But if you want to use more of your mind, more of your decision-making capability, more of your latent genius, you now have another method.

A manager of a computer company has a chance to make a sizable sale to a new company. He has three star salesmen from which to choose. He must select the man best for this critical sale. He reviews the matter objectively. Then he goes to his Alpha level.

At level, he invites the new company's chief executive onto the imaginary scene as his consultant. He asks him, "Is the right salesman Mr. A or Mr. B?" He disconnects and B comes to mind. He then asks him, "Is the right salesman Mr. B or Mr. C?" He disconnects and again Mr. B comes to mind. He assigns Mr. B and the big sale is made.

You can use this method for details at first. See how clairvoyant decisions work for you in using this person instead of that person, in using this color instead of that color, this equipment instead of that equipment. As your skill improves, and your confidence grows, you can graduate to the important situations that can bring you big savings in time.

EDUCATION: NEVER TOO LATE

Why were you not taught how to do this in elementary school? Or high school? Or, certainly in college? The answer is that teachers and professors must learn to do it first, and they were not taught this either.

It has been only in the last five years that interest among educators has been mounting in the implications of right brain–left brain functioning.

A report appeared in *American Psychologist* in 1979 in

which Ann Dirkes of the Education Division, Indiana University–Purdue University, stated that techniques for creative thinking can be applied to academic learning. She felt that educators could make better use of the complementary aspects of the two hemispheres. But, she warned, specific techniques may be needed to transfer to the left brain what the right brain knows.

She was so right. The techniques are in these pages. They are not the first techniques ever devised by man to bring the right brain's subtle information to the left brain's verbalized awareness.

Fortune telling throughout the ages has used crystal balls to divert the conscious awareness and let the message through. The pendulum has been a means of delving below the level of consciousness. Dowsing, more commonly used to find water supplies, has been used also over maps to locate lost persons, mineral veins, and optimum retail outlet locations. The Silva Method depends on no such gadgets. The right brain can get its information to us, if given the chance. The Alpha level is that chance. It is too late to get subjective or clairvoyant training in school. But it is not too late to educate yourself subjectively. School is in session now.

CONNECTION TO A LARGER INTELLIGENCE

Niels Bohr, originator of the atomic theory, referred to an unusual *connection* among all physical phenomena, "though we can only speak of it in images and parables." Bohr was inferring a cosmic factor. Heisenberg spoke of "the almost frightening simplicity and wholeness" which nature reflects.

Another physicist, Arthur Miller, describes the struggle of quantum physicists to define intuition and visualization, which played an important role in the development of the quantum theory, and which also infer a "connection."

By imaging at the Alpha level we tap into this universal wholeness; we connect. At Beta, using our physical senses, we disconnect ourselves from the wholeness and concentrate on the physical.

We need to do both. We need to work in this physical world at Beta, utilizing all of our physical senses. And we need to restore our connections to the wholeness, daily, in order to resonate with that wholeness in a sort of two-way conversation.

When you consider that we have invited an expert into our Alpha senses as a consultant to solve a problem, we are placing ourselves on the receiving end of communication with the wholeness (which I prefer to call Higher Intelligence); and when we create an imaginary scene of a solution to that problem, we are on the sending end of that communication. In effect, we become a creative bridge. Our right hemisphere connects us to the wholeness, our left hemisphere to the separateness.

It all happens at Alpha; the right brain is turned on to take its rightful place alongside the left brain and creative energy is funneled through this bridge from Higher Intelligence to the physical plane.

As you, the clairvoyant executive, function more and more naturally in this manner, the connection improves. Had you been taught how to do this, at least in your final year at the university, by now you would be functioning naturally in this manner.

For a while, it might seem unnatural to you. It does not feel unnatural to me; nor does it feel unnatural to millions of Silva Method graduates who use it not only for their business success, but for better health for themselves and others, for making family decisions, and for increasing their skills in vocations, arts, and sports.

You are going to feel more and more comfortable about going to your Alpha level and programming, as you teach yourself through practice and application. You will find it a "necessity of life" to program daily for harmony, creativity, time management, and solutions. You, too, will be extending the application of this natural human endowment to areas of your life and happiness outside of your business success.

Earlier, we suggested that a cassette tape with your voice might be helpful to lead you to your Alpha level and then on to some positive programming. Here is how to make a tape to help you program for a time-efficient, productive day.

PROGRAMMING FOR A TIME-EFFICIENT DAY

What you relax and listen to can change your behavior. As you relax in your living room, the creamy scoop of ice cream you see in a television commercial, accompanied by an equally creamy voice expounding on its taste pleasures, is changing your behavior. It is also changing the behavior of so many thousands of others that it pays the manufacturer to spend tens of thousands of dollars for the opportunity. Voice alone does the trick for radio commercials.

You are about to listen to a radio "commercial." It has a unique product to sell you. I am sure you will want to buy it—a successful day.

The monologue below should be read into a tape recorder. You can then play the tape in the morning when you first awake. When read slowly, with pauses in the appropriate places, the time required to hear it and program for a time-efficient day will be about eight minutes. Can you afford to spend eight minutes of your activity-packed day to listen to this tape? You bet you can. In fact, you cannot afford not to.

In the absence of cassette tape equipment, you can have a person in your family read the monologue to you each morning that you would like to program. Again, it should be read slowly, without changes of emotion or volume in the voice.

This tape does not include programming for the quick solution to specific time-consuming problems, such as the sale of high-priced real estate, as described earlier in this chapter. That should be done starting at night, on retiring.

This is a general tape for use at the start of a day—a good day indeed.

EIGHT MINUTES TO TRANSFORM A DAY

Here is the monologue to be taped or read (do not read parenthetical material): "Find a comfortable position in your bed. Close your eyes. Turn them slightly upward. Count slowly backwards from 5 to 1—5 . . . 4 . . . 3 . . . 2 . . . 1.

"You can deepen your relaxation by visualizing tranquil scenes. Here are some scenes. A grassy meadow with birds singing and billowy white clouds drifting in a blue sky. See the green grass, the blue sky, the white clouds. Hear the birds singing . . . (Pause) . . . Now a white beach with rolling surf. Hear the sound of the waves . . . (Pause) . . . A flower garden. See the many-colored blossoms. Hold one in your hand. Notice how silky the petal is. Smell the fragrance. See one drop of dew on a petal—just like a diamond in the sunlight, reflecting all the colors of the rainbow.

"Now here are some positive statements for your benefit. Repeat them mentally after me. 'Every time I relax this way, I go deeper, faster' . . . (Pause) . . . 'Positive thoughts held at this level of the mind create benefits' . . . (Pause) . . . 'As a clairvoyant business executive, every day I get better, better, and better' . . . (Pause) . . . 'I always maintain serenity of mind, and a wholesome attitude' . . . (Pause) . . . 'When I place these three fingers together of either hand, my mind functions at a deeper level of awareness.'

"You can deepen your relaxation, this time by counting backwards from 25 to 1. Count mentally with me, visualizing the numbers and feeling yourself getting more and more relaxed. When you reach the count of one, you will be more relaxed. (Slow count) 25 . . . 24 . . . 23 . . . 22 . . . 21 . . . 20 . . . 19 . . . 18 . . . 17 . . . 16 . . . 15 . . . 14 . . . 13 . . . 12 . . . 11 . . . 10 . . . 9 . . . 8 . . . 7 . . . 6 . . . 5 . . . 4 . . . 3 . . . 2 . . . 1 . . .

"You will now use your visualization to picture the activities of the day, seeing the clock, as you go, and seeing time to spare as everything goes smoothly, harmoniously, and productively. Start picturing straight ahead and move each hourly picture to the left.

"It is now (insert hour) o'clock. You are having breakfast with your (family, friends). You feel alert and alive. You are radiant and enthusiastic. See others responding positively to your presence.

"Moving the picture slightly to your left, it is now (insert time one or two hours later) o'clock. You are at your place of business. All preliminary activities are being carried out smoothly and efficiently. You are in control. You feel understanding and rapport with co-workers.

"It is now (insert time one or two hours later) o'clock. See a clock with that time on it, again moving the picture slightly to your left. (Insert what is to happen at that time, in your own words, applying it to your business, in ideal terms). All is going well; and there is time to spare. (Continue for one- or two-hour increments, stating the time, moving the picture to the left, and describing ideal conditions.)

"It is now closing time. (See a clock with that time on it, moving the picture slightly more to the left.) You feel fine, energetic, and enthusiastic. You end the business day with all goals reached and progress made. You radiate appreciation and support to others.

"Prepare to end your session, knowing that you are embarking on a creative and fulfilling day, that you are a competent and skillful executive who surmounts all obstacles, solves all problems, and attains all goals. So be it.

"You will now count from 1 to 5, opening your eyes at the count of 5, feeling wide awake, in perfect health, better than before—1 . . . 2 . . . 3. When you open your eyes at the count of 5, you will feel wide awake in perfect health, better than before—4 . . . 5. Eyes open, feeling wide awake, and great!"

SUBJECTIVE LEARNING PLUS PROGRAMMING

This tape has a dual benefit. As you listen to it, you are learning the procedure to go to Alpha and program for a better day for yourself and your company. You are also doing the actual programming.

After a while, you can free yourself from the rigidity imposed by the tape. You will be able to program in the morning without it. As you acquire additional methodology as described in the opening chapters and in the chapters ahead, you will be able to add these additional steps to your daily programming.

As you continue to program daily in this manner, you will be able to go to your Alpha level any time of day or night for whatever purpose, and program in just moments for positive results.

You will then have caught up to the way you should have been using your mind right along had you been educated in school to use your right brain as well as your left.

RIGHT BRAIN EDUCATION— THEORY AND PRACTICE

If you had been right brain educated, here are some course titles you might have taken:

- "Basic Relaxation and Visualization"

- "Survey of Meditative Techniques"

- "Dynamic Meditation"

- "Basic Creative Imagination"

- "Advanced Visualization and Imagination"

- "Anatomy of Left Brain, Right Brain Functioning"

- "Understanding Brain Waves"

- "Bicameral Thinking at Alpha"

- "Sensing at a Distance"

- "Memory and Precognition"

- "The Creative Aspects of Thought"

- "Enhancing Intuition, Instinct, and Inspiration"

Perhaps by taking all of these courses, you might be awarded a bachelor's degree in clairvoyance. By practicing and implementing the procedures in this book, you will have certainly earned that degree.

As you look at the titles of these courses, they appear to conform to the style of academia. But attending these courses would disclose a shift away from the ordinary academic approach.

Each of these classes would entail experiential activities. Professors and students would talk less and do more. The doing would be relaxing, meditating, visualizing, imagining. There would be listening at the Alpha level. There would be visualizing to remember. There would be experiencing the past and "seeing" the future. There would be telepathy, psychometry, and other right brain sensing experiences.

Students would put their three fingers together. They would program for their own academic success. They might even program for the professor to perform at the right level for their optimum learning.

The typical class would have both subjective learning and programming for its successful conclusion. It would be free of competition and stress. It would be relaxed and easy itself and, because of it, all left brain courses would be more relaxed and easy.

In South Pasadena, California, the private experimental New Age School is integrating four areas for enhanced learning—physical senses, emotions, rational thinking and intuition. The school operates six-week sessions each summer for about 200 students. These students start the day with relaxation exercises. They use the exercises also before tests or other stressful events. They are finding that relaxation makes a difference in learning.

If a class is studying electricity, the students are asked to imagine they are electrons. The use of imagination and fantasizing has not only proven to be motivational for the students, but it also accelerates learning and heightens retention levels.

There are exercises in developing intuition. In one, the students are given a piece of graham cracker to feel, smell, and eat. They are then asked to describe where the rest of the graham cracker is hidden. Barbara Clark, professor of special education at the school said, "They pull in information that is not in their rational abilities." She explained that, as more intuition is used, more develops.

Hallelujah! We are getting there. Would you like to wait for the rest of the world to catch up? Or, would you like to continue your practice and development of clairvoyance now?

DETECTING INFORMATION
OUTSIDE OF RATIONAL ABILITIES

A man was found shot in the cab of his pickup truck. A rifle that he usually carried was beside him. It was determined to be the rifle that killed him. The insurance company would not pay double indemnity, claiming that it was suicide.

An attorney for the family, using the Silva Method, went to his Alpha level. He imagined he saw the shooting. It was not suicide; it was accidental. He asked to "see" the cause. His attention was drawn to a certain part of the rifle. When he ended his session and examined that part of the rifle, he found that there was indeed a defect that caused the rifle to fire itself when in a certain position. The death was ruled an accident and double indemnity was paid.

You are beginning to tap your intuitive powers. You are becoming a clairvoyant executive. These powers are all there now; all you have to do is use them. As you use them, you get better and better. You are able to have information about things going on in your plant or office that your rational thinking abilities might never acquire.

We will be examining additional ways to use your Alpha level for these applications of clairvoyance. Undoubtedly, they will occasionally be useful in managing time more efficiently. But we need to progress sequentially, and these must wait for a future chapter.

Later, you will acquire these additional methods for saving time. But first, you need to have the ability to remove the pressure of time. The pressure of time is a time-consumer.

REMOVING TIME LIMIT PRESSURE

A must be accomplished before B and B before C. There is a deadline for C—90 minutes from now. You make a quick estimate. Required time exceeds available time. You tighten up. It is a tense situation.

I am going to have a hard time convincing you of this, but here goes:

– Tense situations consume more time per unit of accomplishment than do relaxed situations.

– If you react stressfully to a deadline or time limit, your stress interferes with your mental and physical skills. You take more time than you do normally.

– If you take two minutes to relax and program yourself positively, those two minutes are saved many times over. What you are doing, in effect, is taking the sting out of the bee—removing the pressure from the time limit.

Fortunately, in my effort to convince you of this, I have an ally—you. I am going to give you the two-minute method. You are going to test it under stressful conditions. And I will have accomplished my purpose.

If you have been reading this book first, intending to practice later, or if your practicing has not kept up with your reading, you can still use this two-minute stress reliever with positive results now.

A TWO-MINUTE STRESS RELIEVER

The following procedure can be followed in your office, your parked car, the lavatory, or wherever you will not be interrupted. Do not rush it. Take it seriously. Do it as though your life depended on it. (It might.)

• Sit in a chair comfortably. If your belt, tie, or shoes are too tight, loosen them. Make a fist. Tighten it. Let it go. Remember the feeling of letting go. Clench your teeth. Prepare to remember the feeling of letting go. Let go. Do the same with an ankle. Let go. Now close your eyes, take a deep breath and exhale, and turn your eyes slightly upward. Re-create that feeling of letting go in your scalp and forehead. Smooth your brow. Feel that letting go in your eyelids, your face, your jaw. Be aware of your neck and shoulders. Let go there. Let go with your chest and abdomen. Turn your attention to your upper back and let go. Now your lower back. Let go. Now your hips, thighs, knees, legs, ankles, feet, and toes. Let go, in each place. Take a full minute to do this.

Then count backwards from 25 to 1, slowly. Visualize a peaceful place that you can remember—your bed, your favorite chair, your back yard, a meadow, a hill, or beach—any peaceful place you can recall. Pretend that you are there for a few moments. Now repeat mentally to yourself. "Every time I relax this way, I go deeper, faster. Time is my friend. It works for me. When I open my eyes at the count of five, I will be wide awake, feeling fine, confident and in control. One, two, three. When I reach the count of five and open my eyes I will be wide awake, feeling fine, confident and in control. Four, five." Open your eyes. "I am wide awake, feeling fine, confident and in control."

This exercise does not consume two minutes. It *adds* to time. If you do not think time is elastic, try watching for the bus to come or the pot to boil. Compare the feeling of total elapsed time with when you think of more interesting and creative things.

You cannot stop the clock. But you can, in effect, slow it down; be less aware of it. Be relaxed about it. You will meet your "impossible" deadline, with time to spare. And you will live longer.

DEFUSING STRESS FROM LONGER RANGE TIME LIMITS

A doctoral dissertation is an imposing event. Its time limit adds to its stressfulness. Mary K. was concerned. She had postponed starting until she was sure of her research. Now time was too short for comfort. The more she tightened up, the less she progressed. She then used the two-minute stress reliever daily. She finished two days early.

The business manager's routine is filled with short-range time limits and long-range time limits. The two-minute stress reliever helps with all time limits. Use it once for the tight day. Use it daily for the tight week or month. These tight periods then loosen up. You find that what seemed to be not enough time turns out to be more than enough time.

A woman about to give birth is given hypnotic suggestions that the time during contractions will be brief and the time in between contractions will be long. When the contractions begin, they pass "quickly." The time in between is "long" and restful.

The mind can distort time. When we are pressured, it means that we are considering time to be too short, and we are distorting it to be too short. We can reverse the process. We can distort time in the other direction. Our motions then appear to be slow. In effect, we are moving fast without feeling as if we were moving fast; and there is plenty of time.

Add one more step to the two-minute stress reliever for long-range time limits:

- Before ending your session, see a calendar with a date halfway to your deadline. Hold this picture slightly to the left. See the goal more than half reached. Next, move the scene still more to your left, and see the deadline date on your calendar. See the goal reached.

PLANNING AHEAD WITH MORE OF YOUR MIND

For the clairvoyant executive who wishes to schedule his time in a more efficient manner, here is the procedure:

- Go to your level before going to sleep, and program yourself to awaken at the proper time to program yourself most efficiently.
- When you awaken during the night, again go to your level and state mentally that you will be sitting down to work on your schedule the following morning at some time between 9:00 AM and 12:00 PM and that you will then produce an optimum schedule for the most efficient use of your time.
- Remind yourself that while working on developing your schedule, should you be faced with a difficult decision, all you need to do is bring together the tips of the first three fingers of either hand and more of your mind will be brought to bear on the problem.
- Fall asleep from level.

The next morning, when you sit down at your desk to work out your schedule for the future, set up appropriate time units, such as months, weeks, days, mornings and afternoons, or hour by hour. Spell out your assignments for each time slot.

If you are in doubt, put your three fingers together and think about the alternatives. Release your fingers and address yourself again to the alternatives. One alternative will come to your mind as the appropriate choice. Use it.

You may not have any such doubts. In fact, when you sit down to work out your future schedule, you may be surprised at how it all seems to fall into place.

Once you have set up your schedule, let it go for the rest of the day. That night, review it before going to sleep, and reinforce your compliance with it with additional programming as follows, in order to make it automatic, to make it stick:

- Program yourself at level to awaken during the night at the proper time to program yourself most effectively.
- When you awaken during the night, again go to level.
- Review the schedule, mentally noting what you have scheduled for each time slot.
- Permit yourself to fall asleep again from level.

When you begin the scheduled day, you will have an urge to abide by the plan that you have worked out. You will want to comply with what the schedule calls for.

THE HALFWAY POINT

This might be a good place to pause in your reading and let your right brain catch up. This means to continue with the initial fifty days of early morning practice. Then it is advisable that you begin to use visualization and imagination, first in practice sessions, then applying these faculties to actual situations in your business for their solution or resolution.

Use as many of the techniques as seem applicable, as frequently as seems appropriate. Build up experience of success. As you prepare to repeat a technique, remember the last success. If there was a failure, ignore it. If there was a partial success, think of the successful aspects only.

The salesman who remembers the times he was rejected is paving the way for more of the same. The business executive who dwells on his "misses" as a clairvoyant is reinforcing failure.

Remember your success. Go for it again. Reinforce clairvoyance by remembering successes no matter how trivial. As you reinforce success in this manner, you create a climate for greater success.

Your right brain neurons need the practice and encouragement that you have given your left brain neurons.

Do. Accept your success. Do more. Remember, in Chapters 1, 2 and 3, I gave you ways to solve important problems. After fifty days, you can do it.

In the chapters ahead, we do more. We expand our Alpha functioning and apply it to more diverse business manager situations. The clairvoyant executive becomes comfortable with super-normal performances.

Are you ready?

10
Getting the Word to Subordinates, Supervisors, Suppliers, and Salespeople

Research into the abilities of the human mind is escalating around the world. My organization continues to participate in and keep abreast of that research, but, happily, the job is getting more and more difficult. I say happily, because, were the opposite to be true, mankind would be in for an era of "more of the same"—wars, economic woes, full prisons, and burgeoning hospitals.

As agencies of government, health care, education, and industry become more aware of the abilities of the human mind, and mind research is supported, the promise of a better world becomes closer to reality.

One of the major shifts in scientific perception has been in regard to space. Where space was once considered to be "nothingness," it is now perceived to be "somethingness." The vacuum of space, intruded upon by light, cosmic rays, other forms of energy, and, of course, solid bodies, is now looked on not as emptiness but rather as a continuum with properties.

These properties of space, as seen by some scientists, include "agreement," "intent," and the storing and conduction of intelligence. The brain is seen as a hologram, projecting into space what our senses perceive as the universe.

"Empty space is a delusion," states Professor J. Grinberg-Zylberbaum of Universidad Nacional Autonoma de Mexico, writing in *Psychoenergetics.* * "What we call space is in reality an energetic matrix filled with information." He goes on to define experience as the interaction between the brain's neuron field of energy and the quantum field, or space energy field.

"When a neuronal field is capable of interacting with the high syntergic portions of space, the resulting experience will be a holistic and unified one; the observer will experience a state of unification with everything else in the universe.

"Thus," he concludes, "a unified Mind exists and can be experienced."

All of this is expressed in a paper describing a study of human communication, how neuronal fields interact, especially when feelings, thoughts, and emotions are conveyed and shared without the use of verbalization. The EEG equipment was used to measure brain changes during this communication interaction. The evidence pointed to the neuronal fields in interaction reaching an identity and becoming One. The capital O is the good professor's. "Strictly speaking," he concludes, "they are always One."

THE CLAIRVOYANT ONE

When the business manager uses the Alpha level to become clairvoyant and to communicate telepathically, he is partly tuning out his objective separateness and partly tuning in his subjective Oneness.

Oneness is a difficult concept. We are separate people with separate minds, in separate companies or firms, working separately and competitively, going in different directions, to reach separate goals. Nowhere is there a Oneness that our eyes can see, fingers touch, noses sense, or ears detect.

Yet, when we go to Alpha and use the mind to visualize and imagine, the mind produces results that contradict the separateness and confirm the Oneness.

Glenn P. goes to his level and tells his supervisor subjectively that he wishes to be transferred to the day shift. Objective attempts to get such a transfer have failed, despite

---

*Volume 4, pages 227–256, Gordon and Breach Science Publishers, Inc. 1982

his appeals to help save his marriage. The next day he gets the transfer.

What does subjective communication have that makes it succeed where objective communication has failed? The answer can be stated in many ways with different words, but all meaning the same thing. Some of these words could be: Oneness, Higher Self, Togetherness, Higher Intelligence, God.

What word you use to explain the contact is not vital to your success in utilizing the Silva Method. But it is vital to your success to accept the concept of a unity underlying the separation.

The unity exists, whether you accept it or not; but as you feel yourself in rapport with humankind, your clairvoyance improves.

BARRIERS TO SUBJECTIVE COMMUNICATION

The business manager with a perpetual chip on his shoulder is a poor objective communicator. More often than not, he gets "tuned out" by colleagues and subordinates.

The same is true of his subjective communication. He gets "tuned out" by the brain neurons he is attempting to reach. Separateness begets separateness. Togetherness begets togetherness. Communication, objective and subjective, depends on togetherness. You have to talk the other person's language.

Do your subordinates talk your language? How about your supervisors, your suppliers, your salespeople or customers? In a way, is it not true that each talks a different language? The words may not be different, but each sees the world from his vantage point. As the American Indian put it, before you can communicate with another man, "you must walk in his moccasins." This means that you must see things from his point of view.

However, you do not have his point of view. You are a manager. Your point of view is probably more company oriented than that of your subordinates; it is certainly more department oriented. You want your department to come up smelling like roses. Similarly, your point of view is more defensive of your activities when compared to your supervisor's. Your point of view takes on an adversary role with your suppliers and a leadership role with salespeople.

Different points of view mean different sides in controversies, different answers to problems, different concepts of who is right. These differences interfere with objective communication. "Please try to see it from my point of view." "You are being stubborn." "You don't seem to understand."

These differences are bypassed in subjective communication by right brain transmission. When you go to your Alpha level, you leave the role-playing behind. You are relaxed. You visualize and imagine solutions for the good of everybody concerned.

I mentioned this earlier—in subjective communication, *who* is right must be ignored in favor of *what* is right. But it needs to be emphasized.

Most of us fall prey to antagonism, jealousy, hostility, and other personal rivalries or animosities in the competitive business world.

"I can't take him." "He bugs me." "What a b——."

These negative feelings become a part of our life style. We almost enjoy them. We rail against an objectionable person in our conversations with others. We look for support from others in reinforcing each resentment.

The time has come, Mr. Executive, when you can no longer enjoy the luxury of animosity, if you want to enjoy the advantages of clairvoyance. Each animosity or negative feeling is a contributor toward separation and therefore a barrier to oneness.

How then do you proceed? Can an executive expunge himself of jealousy, dislike, or even outright hate? The answer is yes.

HOW TO DISSOLVE THE BARRIERS

It would be a difficult act to agree to do, were I to ask that you go and shake hands with that s.o.b. in the department who has been "gunning" for you. In fact, you probably would not do it. But, would you do it in your imagination? Of course you would, if you thought it would do any good. It would. And that is exactly what I am going to ask you to do.

The "bum" in supply who always delays you; the vice president who always singles you out for criticism; the accountant who is always going over your head; they all need to be on your next subjective communication agenda.

Each needs to be visualized and communicated with. The communication needs to be on a high level of diplomacy and statesmanship as if not only your career depended on clearing the air, but greater things—like the progress of the entire industry, perhaps even world peace (and it might).

The procedure is this: You make a list of these individuals. It is your "hit" list. You are going to hit them with love and understanding. You may want to include a member of your family who is giving you a difficult time, or a friend, or a neighbor. Anybody causing resentment in you needs to be on the list. No matter where the resentment is directed, it is separating you from the universe, interfering with the subjective "connection."

Next, go to your level, list in hand. You can do this when you awaken in the morning. Count down 5 to 1. Turn your eyes slightly upward. "See" the first person. Discuss the problem mentally. Apologize for your part in any misunderstanding. Invite a mutual forgiveness. Move the picture to the left and see it accepted. See a handshake or whatever symbol of rapport is appropriate. Feel relief. Go on to the next person on your list. Program yourself ahead of time that opening your eyes briefly to read a name will not interrupt your Alpha. Complete conversations with all on your list and end the tension.

In the days ahead, monitor these relationships. There should be a difference. Not only will you notice more warmth in your attitude to each, but also more warmth in their attitude toward you.

If resentment persists in any relationship, you need to repeat this exercise at night: Go to bed with the 3-to-1, 10-to-1 method and program to awaken at the appropriate time to communicate with this person. When you awaken automatically, return to your level and go through the same procedure with this person—forgiving and feeling rapport restored, with the scene moved slightly to the left.

Summary

- Make a list of individuals with whom you have an adversary relationship.
- Go to level on awakening in the morning.
- Use the list and talk subjectively with each, creating an understanding and mutual respect, and seeing it take effect on your left.
- Monitor the relationships. If any do not respond satisfactorily, continue at night.
- Before going to sleep, go to level and program to awaken at the ideal time for such programming.
- When you awaken, go to level again and repeat the subjective conversation towards clearing the air. See it accepted, to your left. Feel it.
- Fall asleep from level.

USING THE RIGHT LANGUAGE IN REPORTS

With the clearing of the air, no static can interfere with your communications. Objective communications also improve. But the objective-subjective teamwork that is created by preprogramming the Three Fingers technique is also permitted to function with improved results.

When you sit at your desk to write a memo or report, you are at the Beta level. You review the message you wish to convey. You place it in some logical sequence, perhaps reviewing the events leading up to it—the actions taken, the conclusions reached, the recommendations for implementing those conclusions. Then, you dig in and write.

This is the objective approach. There is nothing wrong with it. But there is something missing. Add that "something" and you have a more effective memo or report.

The "something" is the added benefit of the subjective approach. If memo or report writing combines both the objective and subjective approach, the result is a memo or report that comes alive for the person or persons at whom it is directed. The "something" is the transmission of your brain's right hemisphere.

– It uses the words that are best grasped by all concerned.

– It moves its point of view closer to a consensus.

– It appeals more to the goals and aspirations of everybody.

All of this happens automatically as a direct result of adding the subjective dimension to the process of writing memos and reports—putting right hemisphere input into words.

SUBJECTIVE CONTRIBUTIONS TO WRITING

You can add the subjective dimension to your writing by going to your level at night before falling asleep and programming yourself to awaken at the best time to work on the project.

When you awaken automatically, return to your level and begin to think about the memo or report.

To whom is it going? Does there need to be more than one version of it? What is the purpose? What ground must it cover? How might it be organized? What are its conclusions and recommendations?

As you review these aspects in your mind, answers may come. Some you will have already surmised previously. Others will add new insights. If answers do not come immediately, do not wait. Continue to review the writing project in your mind from start to finish.

Then, program yourself for the Three Fingers Technique by saying, "When I begin to write this report or any report in the future, by simply placing the tips of the first three fingers together of either hand, my full faculties will be brought to bear on the project—my right hemisphere and my left hemisphere, whichever is needed—and I will become aware of the best format, the best words and phrases, and the best ideas to communicate in the simplest and most understandable way. This will take place even with my eyes open."

THE CLAIRVOYANT WRITER

The proof is in the pudding, they say. The book you are reading is in the nature of a long memo combined with an extensive report. It has been written about the Silva Method *with* the Silva Method. I have used my own technique in order to say the right thing at the right time. So has my associate, Dr. Stone. Since he is a professional writer, let us hear how he supplies the subjective approach.

"I have been going to my level and programming for so many years, that I am able to do it just by relaxing and unfocusing my eyes. This I do in the evening, usually before retiring. I sort of daydream about where I am in the writing and where I need to go. I daydream about my next day's schedule. I see myself writing the first few hours of my morning. I see myself writing between one and two thousand words. Then I forget about it. The next morning, so it is. I cover the ground in a relaxed and productive way.

"We have all seen the writer depicted in movies or on television. He is frustrated and tense, tearing sheet after sheet from the typewriter, crumpling them up and slamming them into the wastebasket. That is not a picture of me. My writing flows. I seldom have to rewrite. I am calm and reflective.

"Something else happens. I place reference books on my desk that I believe might be useful for the project on which I am working. I place them on my left, which is not only the future, but the right brain runs the left side of the body. Two months later, I finish the project and find that I have never had to look into those reference books. They act as experts, invited into my imagination, and I get automatic answers to every question that arises. Sometimes I am stumped. I may even have to stop writing an hour or two earlier. Then the mail arrives and there is something in a letter or periodical that is exactly what I need. I may get a phone call from somebody wishing to talk to me about something. Again, it is right on target. The newspaper arrives and there on page . . . Need I say more?"

The clairvoyant executive is a clairvoyant writer. That is because he is doing his thinking at Alpha.

Take a minute now to do a simple test. Find a piece of paper and write a sentence or two, anything that comes to mind, that might have some meaning for you at the moment. Put the book down and do it now. I'll wait.

Fine. Now turn the paper over. Go to your level. Open your eyes and write again—anything that comes to mind, that might have some meaning for you at the moment. Put the book down and do it now.

Now compare what you have just written at Alpha with what you wrote before at Beta. You have probably written a sentence or two at Alpha that has more depth, or more beauty, or more of a philosophical view, or more meaning. Sometimes the difference is only slight; sometimes it is pronounced, depending on the strength of right brain transmission at Alpha and how you mentally approach the informal test.

This is not to suggest that you go to Alpha and try to remain at Alpha while you write. This is not possible. Writing is a Beta activity, and as you begin to write at Alpha, you drift back up to Beta. Before you begin to type at your typewriter keyboard, put your three fingers together. Then begin writing, and whenever you pause, put your three fingers together again. If you are handwriting something, holding pen or pencil in one hand, just keep holding the tips of the first three fingers of the other hand together. In this way, because you have preprogrammed yourself to function—and this pre-programming is essential—both hemispheres are contributing to your report. It makes a difference.

A BETTER COMMUNICATIONS RECEIVER

Part of the daily stress to which managers are subjected is provided by the volume of important material that must be read and remembered. You can use more of your mind, and, as a result, retain more of the information contained in a special report or memo, in the following way:

- Read the report or memo into a tape recorder.
- Then go to your level and listen to the tape at your level.
- Put your three fingers together if you need to memorize parts of the report.
- When the tape is completed, and you have used the Three Fingers Technique, remind yourself that you will remember whatever you need to by again putting your three fingers together.
- End your session and turn off the tape recorder.
- If the report or memo is the subject of a meeting or discussion, read the report or memo once more before the event.

It is not meant that this be standard procedure for all reports and memos, but rather a special procedure for a particularly vital report or memo. It is a valuable procedure when the report or memo is:

1. of considerable length;

2. contains figures, statistics, quotas, or formulae essential to the content;

3. delineates new procedures or programs of some complexity.

The above procedure calls for hearing the report four times—initial reading, reading into the recorder, listening to the recorder, and reading prior to its initial application. The retention factor is multiplied many times more than four. Listening at Alpha could in itself be equivalent to reading at Beta four times or more.

The mind at Alpha is a supermind, able to retain what it hears—more accurately, longer, and with easier recall.

THE BICAMERAL SPEAKER

Speaking is also a Beta activity. You are not likely to be able to give a talk, a lecture, or an explanation to an audience (of one or many) at the Alpha level without drifting up to

Beta. Again, the Three Fingers Technique comes to the rescue. Again, it makes a difference.

Up until now, shop-floor supervisors have been barking out orders like drill sergeants—management by shouting. Today, a growing number of companies are beginning to find that it just does not work any more. A new type of training is being instituted that is turning shop-floor supervisors from crack-that-whip bullies into more understanding bosses. This training embraces such about-face approaches as "Calmly describe the employee's behavior that concerns you" and "Express reassurance and support."

Calmness and support are right brain characteristics. The training thus adds a right brain approach to the shop-floor supervisor's repertoire. Will it help? Of course it will. How can it miss? More of his brain is working for him.

According to a report in *Time* Magazine*, Fairchild Republic Co., in its Farmingdale, N.Y. plant, had a morale problem when it had to lay off 1,000 workers. It then sent nearly 100 supervisors through a privately sponsored training program for understanding workers, and giving calmness and support to them. The morale of the work force began to improve. It moved ahead of its production schedules. It later won the Air Force productivity award.

Getting the word to other people needs to be a bicameral brain activity. And it can be, thanks to the Alpha level.

WEST MEETS EAST

The Japanese worker is outproducing the American worker. There is growing interest by American business leaders in the Japanese system, how it differs, and why it works. When they examine the system, they do not find what they expect to find. They do not find new and stronger incentive programs. They do not find tighter control and harsher discipline. They do not find a heightened spirit of competition.

What they find instead is difficult to categorize in standard western business competition terms. It is more subtle, more ephemeral. It is a group attitude, a collective feeling, something we might call teamwork. Each individual has a dedica-

---

*June 7, 1982.

tion not only to self and family, but also to company and country. It is not exactly something that the western businessman, visiting Japan, can package and take back to his company. What he is witnessing is the bicameral brain at work. It not only competes, it cooperates.

The left brain figures out what to do and how to do it at the nitty gritty level, while the right brain maintains a connection to the group and its overall needs. The result: individuals acting in concert. Measured on the profit and loss statement, it makes beautiful music.

This bicameral approach to management can be packaged. It is packaged now. It is called the Silva Method.

THREE FINGERS TALK

When you have preprogrammed the Three Fingers Technique and use it in a conversation with an employee, the conversation moves in a clearly identifiable direction.

By putting your three fingers together, you have activated the right hemisphere, and it is taking its rightful place alongside your left hemisphere in your conversation. You are functioning bicamerally. With the right brain participating, your left brain dominated thinking is now balanced thinking. Imbalance is corrected.

Characteristics of that imbalance recede. You might call them the five deadly sins of leadership:

1. Arrogance. A tendency to claim credit for yourself but give little to others

2. Pride. An overwhelming sense of one's importance

3. Haughtiness. Feeling a high regard for yourself but a poor regard for others

4. Vanity. An intense desire for admiration and praise

5. Disdain. Feeling contemptuous of the inferiority of others compared to yourself

Rare is the manager who can claim total freedom from all five of these traits. They come with the job. Each is a formidable impedance to having more of your mind working for you. Each is a block to communicating successfully.

Put your three fingers together and these impedances and blocks are circumvented. You speak in a more acceptable way because you have separated yourself less.

Dr. Robert P. Levoy, author of *The Successful Professional Practice** and popular conductor of day-long seminars on this subject with professional groups throughout the country, advocates a humanized practice. He deplores the "ivory tower" into which many professionals place themselves. Come out from behind that desk, he says, and sit "knee to knee, eyeball to eyeball" with your client.

Any change from separateness in the direction of mutuality is a change for the better—better human relations, yes, but also better productivity, better efficiency, better financial results.

It is difficult to make such changes by willpower. It is easy to make such changes by programming for them at Alpha: "Every time I put the tips of the first three fingers of either hand together, my mind works at a deeper level of awareness, and my right brain hemisphere transmission takes place."

While speaking, let the tips of those three fingers touch, and your words will touch others.

PUBLIC SPEAKING SOLUTIONS

Your expenses have been paid by the company to attend a seminar. Now you are being asked to talk to an audience of managers and supervisors to share the salient points of that seminar. The time has come. Your heart is beating harder and faster. Your palms are sweating. Your knees are weak and shaking, as you approach the lectern. Fear of public speaking strikes nine out of ten people and does not go away easily.

Professor Lauren Ekroth of the Speech Department, University of Hawaii, is a Silva Method graduate. He provides his students with an effective procedure for dealing with those symptoms that precede the act of public speaking. His

---

*Prentice-Hall, Inc., Englewood Cliffs, N.J., 1970.

method includes deep breathing, affirmations, and reinforcement.

Advance affirmations, made at a relaxed level, include, "I can develop a plan to deal with it." Affirmations and actions at the moment of being introduced include, "Take a slow, deep breath—ah, good," and "Relax. I am in control." Later, he suggests such reinforcing affirmations as, "It worked. I was able to do it" and "It gets better and better each time." It does work; and it does get better and better.

Before your talk, you can do some preprogramming to prevent those fear-of-public-speaking symptoms:

1. Preprogram that tapping the thymus with your three fingers and putting a smile on your face will make you feel more confident.

2. Preprogram that by putting the tips of the first three fingers together of either hand, you will immediately know what to say.

3. Preprogram that by taking a deep breath and exhaling slowly, you will be calm and in control.

By taking these actions you become in control. You can enhance that control with positive affirmations at Alpha, along the Ekroth lines, before and after the public speaking event.

GETTING THE MESSAGE TO GROUPS

When there is a group of people to whom he must give a talk of an expository nature—explaining how to perform a new plant operation, for example—the manager can do an effective job of getting the message across in a way that can be thoroughly assimilated by the staff, or he can do an ineffective job that leads to delays and errors.

Confining this communications project to objective means alone increases the chances of ineffectiveness. Reinforcing this communications project with subjective means decreases the chances of ineffectiveness. In fact, it assures the message getting through.

How to Communicate Subjectively to a Group

- Before going to sleep the night before, go to your level and program to awaken at the right time to speak to the group subjectively.
- When you awaken during the night, again go to your level. You are now at the right dimension of mind to "broadcast" (right hemisphere transmission) to the group, as you would over a loudspeaker or public address system.
- Imagine the group to whom you will be speaking the next day. See them listening attentively to the public address system.
- Imagine you are speaking to the group. Cover all the points you will be covering objectively the next day.
- Go to sleep from your level.

Optional

- After completing your imaginary talk, move the scene slightly to the left and see the workers performing their new tasks perfectly.
- Move the scene slightly more to the left and see awards and citations being made for excellence in production.

On the following day, give your talk objectively. It will be effective.

Conversation is always more effective when first done subjectively, and then objectively.

SPECIAL ONE-TO-ONE EFFECTIVENESS

You are probably faced with the need to get through to individuals more frequently than to groups. And you are probably quite aware of how difficult this is at times. You get nods of the head. You get "Yes." You get "I understand." You get "No problem."

Then it turns out there is a problem. Either you were talking in a foreign language, or the person to whom you were talking was pretending to be awake. You have to take your time and the time of others affected by the problem to repeat the instructions. Even then, there will be no guarantee that the message is getting through.

There is another way. Let us say that a new employee has been introduced to you and is being shown the plant. Tomorrow you will meet with her first thing in the morning to explain her duties and responsibilities. Meanwhile, here is what you do:

- At night before falling asleep, you, the clairvoyant manager, go to your level and instruct yourself to awaken at the appropriate time to communicate with the new subordinate and outline the duties.

- When you awaken during the night, again go to your level and visualize the new subordinate. (If you have not yet met the new subordinate, imagine what she might look like. You do not have to see her face. Merely outline the body.)

- Talk to the new subordinate at this subjective level. Outline the duties, step by step. Talk to her as an equal, not as a superior. Be helpful.

- Next, move the scene slightly to the left of its position in front of you. See the new employee working at her duties. She is doing well on the job. She is performing her responsibilities capably and efficiently.

- Again, move the scene slightly to the left. It is now a year or more into the future. The employee is getting promoted. She is being recognized for a job well done.

- You, the clairvoyant manager, then go to sleep from your level.

- The next day, before explaining the duties to the new subordinate in person, at the objective or Beta level, take a moment to unfocus your eyes and recall the two future scenes of the night before. See the person doing the job well—picturing a little to the left. Then, further to the left, see the person being rewarded at a future time. And this will be so.

TALKING SUBJECTIVELY OVER DISTANCES

I need to talk for a moment to your left hemisphere. If I do not make a logical case for what I am about to present, your left brain will reject it out of hand. And you will be deprived of a valuable managerial communications tool.

We have come a long way since smoke signals. Satellites help us send messages instantaneously around the world. If you had said this was possible a century ago, you would have been thought of as having "lost your marbles."

Believe me, some people still react as though I am living in a world of delusion when they hear me say, "Go to your level; see your friend on the other side of the world; and explain what needs to be done." As far as science has come, the concept of energy traversing long distances is still a difficult one for us to accept, especially when the energy we are using is the right hemisphere of our brain's psychotronic energy—the energy of consciousness.

Brain neurons resonate to other brain neurons no matter where in the world they are.

Remember the discussion of Cleve Backster's work with plants and how their communication receptivity was registered on the polygraph equipment? Well, that research was carried forward by Japanese scientists who developed electronic equipment that could detect communication being sent at the plant level, directionally.

One day, these scientists broke for lunch leaving the equipment pointed to the sky. When they returned, they found a readout showing communications had been received at the plant level. They moved the equipment around, still pointed skyward, and found several points where communications at the plant level were arriving from outer space.

This obviously surprised them. But it did not surprise us in the Silva Method organization. We know that humans can communicate over vast distances, so why not plants? We do it every day.

THE LIMITS OF SUBJECTIVE COMMUNICATION

The right hemisphere connects us to a nonmaterial realm. The subjective realm is timeless and spaceless. In other words, subjective communication is instant and is not affected by distance. Can you "talk" subjectively to your salesman working thousands of miles away in Honolulu? Yes. Can you "talk" subjectively to a supplier in Pittsburgh, hundreds of miles away? Yes. Can you "talk" subjectively to an associate in London, England? Yes.

You can communicate subjectively to these distant people in the same way as you just "talked" to your new subordinate in the plant in order to better get across his duties and responsibilities.

However, just as the right brain is not meant to be a substitute for the left brain, but rather an adjunct to it, subjective communication should not be used as a substitute for objective communication, but rather as an aid to it.

Will you be phoning the salesman in Honolulu? Before you do, go to your Alpha level as previously described, and hold the conversation in your imagination. Later, the long-distance call at the Beta level will be more readily understood and accepted.

Will you be sending a telex to the Pittsburgh supplier? Send the message by subjective means first, and see how much more quickly you get response and cooperation from your telex later.

Will you be cabling your London associate? Use the Alpha level first, paving the way for positive response from your associate.

The subjective communication should always get through; but there are exceptions.

You already know some of these exceptions. You know, for instance, that talking down, criticizing, or in other ways creating a polarity will break the subjective connection. You know that you must speak on a statesmanlike level, pushing not for who is right, but what is right, and aiming for solutions that will benefit everybody concerned.

That is the subjective realm language. When you follow it up with objective specifics, these specifics will then fit more appropriately into the picture.

There is another exception. If you inject a mass of left brain information into your right brain communication, it can also break the connection. A bunch of facts, a myriad of figures, or dates, times, schedules and formulae—this is all left brain stuff. Rather than go over this while at your level (and it is difficult to stay at Alpha thinking about such Beta stuff), use your Alpha level to speak generally about the importance of this information and how it will be for the benefit of you both that this information be carefully reviewed on receipt.

If you were to talk in a subjective way at the objective level, you would also run into difficulties. Imagine your foreman's reaction, if you were to say, "We need to pull together to make this a better world to live in." He'd probably think you were ready for an extended vacation.

Subjective communication requires its way, objective its way. Although these ways are different, together they build a bridge that spans differences in two minds.

– It could be a difference of opinion.

– It could be a difference in location.

– It could be a difference in vested interest.

The clairvoyant manager using subjective-objective communication always gets through better.

11

How to Make Your Presence More Effective at Meetings and in Other Situations

John and Rita Donahue are two talented young people who are building a successful manufacturing business using Silva Method techniques. Their product—wind chimes.

With John as the hardware expert and Rita as the artist, they started as a hobby in 1973 with weekend sales of under $1,000. In 1975, sales reached $20,000. In 1978, their sales topped $100,000. In 1979, with sales approaching $200,000, the Donahues moved from upstate New York to San Diego, California.

By programming for a smooth move, their business did not miss a beat. Sales have continued to increase for their company, Magic Wind. Rita went through the Silva Method training courses in San Diego to heighten her creative abilities. New products were needed to satisfy the increasing demand. As a result of that review, a "tremendous spurt of creative, new ideas came."

Animal wind chimes were created and named "Animal Clackers." "Bottom Line" chimes were born, with $1 at the top and a descending spiral of 0-added denominations—$10, $100, $1,000—all the way to $1,000,000. And that is the annual sales figure that they are currently programming for.

Would you like to bet against their reaching it? If I were a betting man, I would give odds that they will reach it.

"There is no way to estimate the value of Mind Control principles in the conduct of a business," they recently wrote me. "The power of the deep levels of the mind to solve practical problems, bring forth creative new product ideas, and develop positive employer-employee relationships is fantastic and vital."

Marcus Aurelius said 1800 years ago, "Our life is what our thoughts make it." This is true, even with thoughts uncontrolled. It is especially true when you control your thoughts.

We hope that you have begun your practice of controlling your mind and getting a "handle" on the Alpha level; or that you are in the process of taking or planning to take the Executive 30-Hour Silva Method Course for a more accelerated training.

Either way, you are approaching a new level of professionalism as a business executive. You are activating more of your mind to do your job. Even if you do your job as you are now doing it—at Beta—you will show an improvement. However, the greatest leap in ability will occur because you will also be doing it when necessary at Alpha.

THE RANGE OF ALPHA SKILLS

We began this text by selecting certain basic management responsibilities and showing how the Alpha level can be used to assist you in these matters. As we progress, the versatility of Alpha becomes evident. Your need to lessen responsibilities by cutting functional slices out of your managerial day becomes less. If you know how to program for better communications, you know how to program also for better outcomes, for better relations, for better solutions.

There is no limit. The Beta divisions are not required by Alpha. The mind at Alpha is not pigeonholed. It transcends all separations, as functional as those separations appear to be.

Alpha applications form a spectrum that embraces all managerial functions, all business, all of living.

To build Magic Wind, the Donahues used the Alpha level to boost sales, create new products, generate new ideas, communicate subjectively with workers, solve cash flow problems, find suitable locations, and scores of other things. But contrast these many applications to the use made by this Silva Method lecturer.

Dean Winkler, 27, of Kansas City, Missouri, was driving his sports car when it slammed into a tree and rolled down into a gully so thick with brush that it was hidden from view, according to a story in the *Weekly World News*. While Dean was unconscious in the wreck, his family searched for him for two days without success. Then they turned to a man whose name they had known from the newspapers because he had helped police solve several crimes—Randy Youmans, Silva Method lecturer.

Youmans went to his level, projected to Winkler by imagining him and proceeded to describe the crash scene in such detail that rescuers were able to rush to the spot, just in time to save Winkler's life.

Using this application as an example, and using programming to reach a million-dollar volume as another example, how many other applications fit in between? They are countless; as many as you can think of. The mind can do anything.

THE RANGE OF SILVA METHOD TECHNIQUES

There may be many ways to activate the mind to do anything. The anatomy of the brain dictates that all of these ways, however, must use the Alpha level.

Primitive man must have paused in his hunt for game. He must have listened, looked, even smelled for some clue as to which direction to move. In the absence of such objective clues, he must also have imagined in which direction to move. He was then "moved" to go in a direction that yielded results. And he survived. He survived without the Silva Method.

The Silva Method is a way of restoring faculties that mankind once used more frequently than now. It does not claim to be the only way; but it is a thoroughly researched way that has been found successful. It uses the Alpha level. It uses words and pictures to program at the Alpha level. This might be considered generic—that is, of universal application.

Elements Special to the Silva Method

- The simple way to go to Alpha
- The use of sleep to select the right time to program, both from the standpoint of your own brain as well as the brain or brains with which you are subjectively communicating
- The use of imagined scenes to create them
- The moving of those scenes from straight ahead successively to the left to indicate future results
- Self-triggering techniques, such as the Three Fingers Technique, thumping the thymus with a smile on your face, taking a deep breath
- Triggering techniques for another person, such as drinking liquid, hearing you speak a key word

If the Silva Method required you to go to your level in the middle of a conversation in order to benefit from your subjective mind, it would not be very practical.

"Just a moment, John. In order to tell you what I have to tell you, I must switch mental gears."

Possible, yes. Practical, no. So, we devised a methodology that obviates the need for you to take deep breaths, or close your eyes, or be at Alpha during critical moments in your managerial day. You avoid this by preprogramming and by triggering techniques.

We recommend preprogramming at night. But if there is no intervening night, if the critical event is just hours or minutes away, program anyhow. Program in your office, in the lavatory, or wherever you can enjoy a few minutes of uninterrupted quiet. It is better to program for success at a time less than optimal, than not to program at all.

CONTRIBUTING EFFECTIVELY TO STAFF MEETINGS

You can program, prior to any act or event, to make that act or event more constructive, more productive, more successful. You already know the basics. From here on, I am going to supply ways to utilize the basics in specific ways, so that you can begin to see the versatility of those basics and to be able to apply them not only in standard situations, but also when the "chips are down," in some unusual or unexpected way.

Let's take a standard situation—a meeting. It may be a sales meeting, department heads meeting, or a staff meeting of any sort. It may be an outside seminar, or workshop; a community meeting; a trade organization meeting. You name it.

By now you know to go to your level and to program to awaken at the best time to deal with this meeting. When you awaken automatically, here is what to do at your level:

- Visualize the meeting place and the people you know will be there. If either the location or people are unknown to you, imagine what it or they might look like.

- Make a short talk. Tell the group that you will participate in the meeting the following day, and that you intend to do so with the best of your knowledge; to function in a manner that will contribute to the good of everybody; and that you do so with all sincerity to be of service.

- See the next scene slightly to the left. Now you are in the group. You blend well. You are in rapport with the others, and they with you. They feel good about your presence.

- See the next scene slightly more to the left. The meeting is ending. It has been successful. The group is satisfied with the result. You are shaking hands or commending others, and they you.

- You fall asleep from level.

ENHANCING YOUR EFFECTIVENESS IN PERSONNEL SITUATIONS

There are times when a single programming does not apply to a situation, because it is an ongoing type of event. Let us say, for example, that you have a draftsman who is preparing an elaborate set of working drawings from your sketches and instructions.

You would program at night, before your first contact with him on this project. You would go over the project subjectively just as you will be going over it the next day objectively. The result will be that the draftsman will get the message more thoroughly than he would without your subjective session.

But, you need not stop there. Whenever you have reviewed his progress, that night again program to awaken at the right time. When you do, again go to your level and discuss the project at its present stage. Correct any discrepancies and guide him in the next phase. Thank him for his progress.

Use repeated nightly Alpha sessions to see this project through to its successful conclusion.

If you have more than one project to work on at night and you program to awaken at the best time to program these projects, your mind will automatically select a time that may be somewhat less than optimum for each but which is the best time considering all of them—a sort of vector analysis or averaging. It is the same as when you program to awaken at the best time to program a group situation. The time you automatically awaken is the best time—on the average, remembering that your mind is a key mind in the situation and perhaps controlling the time more than others.

An alternative would be to program to awaken twice or three times—the best time to work on each project. When you awaken the first time, ask yourself, at level, which project to work on. Disconnect. The first project that comes to mind is the one to work on. Do the same the next time you awaken, if there is still more than one project.

We in business have a multiplicity of problems to face constantly. It does not pay to lie awake all night working on them at the Beta level. Nor does it pay to lie awake all night working on them at the Alpha level. Set your priorities—and get a good night's sleep.

ALPHA WORK FROM A TO Z

You can use the same nighttime programming to solve a problem where no particular person or group of persons is necessarily involved in the problem or in its solution.

Brain neurons can resonate with other brain neurons or they can resonate with inanimate matter. It is easier for us to work at the human level than it is at animal, plant, or inanimate levels. But where survival is at stake, all obstacles are quickly crossed by the brain neurons which are fundamentally programmed for survival.

An aircraft engine plant inspector on the West Coast whose job it is to spot defects in the engines by using electronic equipment, is able to unfocus his eyes, imagine that the next engine on the line has arrived, and check it out in his imagination. When he spots a defect in his mental picture, it shows up electronically later.

You can use this unfocusing of the eyes to go to level any time of the day for heightened perception. But working on inanimate problems subjectively is likely to be more successful, at least at the start, if done at night. Here are the steps, once you have wakened automatically and gone to your level:

- See the problem, the machine not working, the response not arriving from overseas, the inanimate situation that needs to be corrected.

- Move the scene slightly to the left. See a correction beginning to take place.

- Move the scene slightly more to the left. See the situation as restored to normal. Everything is normal, better than before.

We are likely to be somewhat shaken up by the results. They are not logical. They are not scientific. They are not explainable by standard means.

What explanation can be given when:

– An intermittent problem becomes less "mittent" and more "inter" and finally disappears altogether?

– A most unlikely person comes up with an ingenious substitute for a missing part?

– A "lost" shipment shows up the next morning?

– A stranger appears with exactly what is needed?

– A flash of insight permits you to take a totally new tack or approach that turns out to be successful?

All we can say is "coincidence."

My definition of coincidence is: "When Higher Intelligence lends a hand to the picture but does not autograph it."

YOUR VERSATILE FINGERS

Once you have preprogrammed that by placing together the tips of the first three fingers of either hand, your mind works at a deeper level of awareness, you have another versatile tool.

You are not limited to using the Three Fingers Technique only in the kind of meeting, talk, or special situation prior to which you did the programming. You can use it whenever you need to be closer to being a genius—and it works. You experience more "coincidences."

Again, what other explanation can be given when, after putting your three fingers together:

– You make some shocking discovery?

– You find a lost item?

– You arrive at a spot in the plant or warehouse just in time to prevent a loss or accident?

– You get a parking place?

– You say something that evokes exactly the information for which you have been digging?

Higher Intelligence sounds like a religious term. But Higher Intelligence is now being recognized by more and more scientists. It is the only concept that can help to explain what they see through microscopes and telescopes. And it is the only concept that can explain what you and I are able to do when we function in both the subjective and objective realm. Alpha is our doorway to Higher Intelligence.

Have you paused to consider whether to say "yes" or "no" to a request? Put your three fingers together.

Do you need to select a person to do a special job and there are several possibilities? Put your three fingers together. The answer that comes is the right one. Accept it.

The more you use your three fingers, the better they will work for you. Why? That simple act becomes a more familiar signal to your brain neurons and your own expectation and belief is heightened with each success.

CONTROL OVER CIRCUMSTANCES AND MATTER

Inanimate matter cannot program, but it can be programmed. Witness our computers. Plants and animals cannot program, but they can be programmed. Witness the effects of human thought on plants in experiments being conducted largely as a result of the Backster effect and of the popularly known Findhorn, Scotland project. Witness the effects of your own thought on your pets.

Only man can do the programming. Only you and I have the ability to program ourselves, others, and even animals, plants and inanimate matter. That makes us special on this planet, does it not? It makes us somewhat like the Creator—like Higher Intelligence.

Through our desire, belief and expectancy, when functioning at ten cycles per second, we can alter conditions in matter near and far. We are amazing creatures.

Mr. Clairvoyant Manager, you merit a raise. You are more influential than you dreamed possible. You are invaluable. All you need to do is use your Alpha level daily in as many ways as you can think of. You can catapult yourself to the top of the company, and your company to the top of the industry.

You are in control. You are in control of your circumstances, in control of your good fortune, in control of your life.

PROGRAMMING FOR SOLUTIONS

Ed Bernd, now on our Laredo staff, had to sell his house in Florida. His real estate agent advised him to lower the asking price, but he was convinced that it was fair. He programmed to awaken at night at the best time to contact a buyer. When he awoke automatically, he imagined a buyer, without seeing a face (seeing a particular potential customer could create a problem for that person and negate the programming), and subjectively explained the reasons why the house was a solid buy. He added that he needed to complete the sale in ten days.

It took seven days for the real estate people to get the word out. Two days later the house was sold at the price he wanted—one day ahead of his programming.

Bette Taylor, early in her business career, programmed to have a dream that would tell her whether to stay in her job as line supervisor or make a change. For two weeks she dreamt of the man who swept the plant floors. Then she understood the dream: Make a clean sweep. It took her a while to act on it, but it was the needed breakthrough in her meteoric business career.

A Canadian attorney who needed to expand his clientele programmed to awaken at the appropriate time at night to deal with this problem. When he awoke he went to his level and visualized his phone ringing and clients contacting him. Within three days, he was called by several people who needed legal assistance in a new area of law in which he had been thinking of specializing and which now has become his main practice.

Bonnie S., an artist, completed the Silva Method Course in July, and by October, programming every day for more commissions to paint portraits, had tripled her income.

We are all problem solvers. One day we may find out that Higher Intelligence has created us for that very purpose—to solve problems—and that business managers have attained their positions because they are superior problem solvers.

We can all be better problem solvers by activating the right hemisphere of our brain to join in. We can all be better problem solvers using the Alpha level and the Silva Method.

Nothing in this text should be interpreted to mean that you can solve only this type of problem or that type of problem. If it is a problem, it has a solution.

Catch-22 situations, "insoluble" problems, and "you're-damned-if-you-do-and-damned-if-you-don't" impasses are Beta stuff. At Alpha, they can be dissolved.

PROGRAMMING FOR PROBLEMS

Unfortunately, programming can also take place at Beta. It takes plenty of repetition but eventually it takes effect. Negative ideas, held in the mind as a matter of habit or way of life, become programming. Statements habitually made become programming.

The man on the production line who is always complaining is contributing to his own unhappiness. The manager who is always saying, "We can't," is contributing to limitations. How about these common statements:

"We don't see eye to eye."

"They don't really care about my ideas."

"He never understands."

"He is just waiting for me to make a mistake."

"They make me sick."

"Oh, my aching back."

"We'll never make it."

"It can't be done."

"Business is so terrible."

"I'm not good at . . ."

These are just ten examples of the kind of programming that saturates our language. It is programming for problems. The Beta world is a world of dichotomy. It thrives on opposites. Its very existence depends on opposites— the negative electron and positive nucleus of the atom. Therefore, it thrives on conflicts, indecisions, pros and cons.

The Alpha world is a world of solutions. It opens up the door to the subjective realm—the realm of solutions. It is a positive realm; a creative realm.

The business manager who uses the Alpha realm to produce solutions can interfere with the manifestations of those solutions by programming at Beta for the continuation of the problem.

Watch your thinking. Watch your words. If you find you are

thinking in negative terms, mentally repeat, "Cancel, cancel."

If you find yourself mouthing negative clichés, or others doing so audibly in your presence, say aloud, "Cancel! Cancel!"

"DOLLAR-A-YEAR MEN" TO ADVISE YOU

I have given you a number of instances where it is helpful to call in experts to answer your subjective questions. The specific instances I have given you are not the beginning and the end. There are hundreds of "Dollar-a-Year" men standing by to be your advisors or consultants. All you have to do is invite them into your Alpha level and ask. They will send you no bills.

They make up a Silva Method technique that helps our brain neurons overcome the separation programming that we are constantly provided in the material world. The "expert" facilitates our connection to Higher Intelligence where all solutions reside.

Whenever you awaken automatically at night to solve a special problem, you can create a duplicate of an individual whom you respect or look up to in the area of expertise you need. Placing that expert in your imagined scenes gives you the opportunity to ask for advice with the special problem.

You do this by directing your question mentally at the expert, then clearing your mind for a moment. When you begin again to think of the problem, an answer comes.

It may feel as if you are making it up. It may feel as if you are putting words in the expert's mouth, as if it is your answer, not his. That is the correct feeling. Accept it. Be sure to thank your consultant before going to sleep from your level.

You may create a duplicate of your leading competitor, of a top attorney, of a high-priced market consultant, of a government expert, of a religious leader, even of a historical figure.

The only difficulty is really remembering that we can do this. We plow ahead forgetting that we can ask an expert.

Cancel, cancel.

HELPING INDIVIDUAL EMPLOYEES

The typical business manager evaluates her employees. She then holds these employees in that framework of capability. The mention of the name of that employee triggers the bad, average, or good "tag" that has been placed on that person.

The clairvoyant business manager knows better. She knows that such judgment creates an expectation and belief which programs the employee to live up to that judgment. Where the judgment is negative, the employee is being programmed negatively.

The answer is not to close your eyes to lack of skill, absence of motivation, or any other negative factor. The answer is to reject it as the status quo, and instead to consider it as a problem looking for a solution.

The solution can be found tonight, at your level:

- When you program to awaken at the right time and then awaken, you again go to level.
- You visualize the employee who needs help in succeeding at what is expected of him.
- This first scene is directly in front of you. You speak to the employee and explain the requirements. You show where improvement is needed and demonstrate to the employee how that improvement can be attained.
- Move the next scene slightly to your left. The employee is doing what he has been told to do. He is performing in an improved way, so improved that he merits your praise. He is happier at his work.
- The third scene is slightly more to the left. The employee is highly successful and valuable to the company. And this is so.

The next day, you do objectively what you have done subjectively. It may not be as directly on an "I'll show you" basis. But, diplomatically, as you customarily explain to employees, you cover the same ground.

A week later, there may be a logical follow-up to that employee's progress. Now that he has gotten this far, he can progress further. So, again you program at night for the employee's receptivity to your instructions, as you did with the three scenes above. And again, the next day, you cover that ground objectively with that employee.

If there are teams, or small groups, that work together, you can program the team in the same fashion and also continue that programming so that the team continues to increase its skill and effectiveness.

HANDLING AN UNEXPECTED EMERGENCY

What do you do if two workers get into an argument and barge into your office to settle it? What do you do if your best customer arrives in a huff because he has found an item to be defective? What do you do if your supervisor calls you to his office to explain an oversight?

Do you say, "Excuse me while I go to my level"? Do you try to put it all off until you have time to consult an expert that night? Do you put a smile on your face and thump your thymus? Of course not.

I repeat: nothing in this text describing the uses and applications of the Three Fingers Technique is meant to limit that technique to those specific uses and applications.

The Three Fingers Technique, once you have preprogrammed it, is a "Johnny on the spot" technique. By triggering all of your mental faculties to go to work, you are equal to any emergency situation. By placing the tips of the first three fingers together of either hand, you have your subjective and objective faculties working for you—and that's quite a team.

Your reaction to the emergency will be calm and considered. You will be in control. You will say the best that there is to be said. You will do the right thing. Ideas will come that will alleviate, substitute, or generate—whatever is called for.

Looking back at the way you handled the emergency situation, you will be impressed. After all, half of the brain is always impressed at what the whole brain can do.

Put your three fingers together looking back, and it will seem "run of the mill."

RESEARCHERS CONFIRM ALPHA PROBLEM SOLVING

Recently, Frederick J. Bremner, Ph.D., and Susan D.C. Russo, M.A., both of Neurophysiology Laboratory, Trinity University in San Antonio, Texas, working with our consultant, Richard E. McKenzie, Ph.D., performed an experiment with ten volunteer university students.

A simple information-processing task was given to the students via a computer-driven television-type screen. The computer screen presents the task. The student responds by pushing one of the five buttons. Another task is presented, then another, faster and faster, until the student can no longer respond or misses the correct button twice in a row. It then flashes, "End of session. Your score was (reaction time). Thank you!"

The students were prepared for this project by being given basic relaxation training, orientation on the procedures, and practice time on the information processing task.

They also understood that their brain waves would be monitored—left and right hemispheres—as part of the research procedure.

The results of the project are that controlled relaxation shows an increase in Alpha production. As the requirement to process information is initiated, the second hemisphere of the brain is activated. The differences in brain wave patterns between the two hemispheres begin to diminish as performance level increases.

"Going to level," conclude the researchers, "may be an important step in the enhancement of man's greatest asset—the ability to solve problems."

NONMANAGERIAL APPLICATIONS

This is a book designed to assist in the training of clairvoyance for business managers.

To be as helpful as possible, we have categorized managerial activities and then delineated how the Silva Method techniques can be applied to those specific categories.

In this chapter, I have attempted to diffuse the applications so that the clairvoyant manager realizes the full spectrum of uses to which the techniques can be put.

The resulting picture has been, I hope, that every aspect of the manager's job can benefit from the Silva Method. There is no managerial situation that cannot be handled in a superior manner with *more* of the manager's mind working on it.

Unfortunately, we have learned how to address ourselves to the job with *less* of our mind working on it. We can stay out all night and show up half awake. Or, we can have a three-martini lunch and return to our desk intoxicated. Or, we can come to work under the influence of drugs.

We know that when we address ourselves to our jobs handicapped in this way, we are less productive, efficient, and creative.

So, it is no great leap in logic to conclude that with more of our minds, not less, we are more productive, efficient, and creative.

This is true whether we are on the job or off the job. That is the final point I wish to make before we begin our final chapter.

The Silva Method puts you in control of your managerial life. It also puts you in control of your private life.

You need to have heightened problem-solving abilities in your private life as much as you do in your professional or business life.

So, once more we eliminate a category. Your business life does not require one method and your private life another. The Silva Method helps you in the office *and* in the home. We state this categorically.

Program for things to go well at home. Help your spouse, not just an office worker. Help your children, too. Program for better health, greater happiness, increased accomplishments. Communicate your love and concern subjectively and objectively. Do the same for yourself.

There are times when using more of your mind through positive imaging at the Alpha level will help you handle stress, make better buying judgments, and induce harmony in private life relationships.

You can write your own ticket. The destination can be a successful managerial career—period. Or, it can include a longer and happier life.

12

Managing with Enhanced Perception in These Times of Change

A repeated nonwinner in the pro ski racing circuits took the Silva Method training and it made a difference. Goeff Bruce, 29, of Burlington, Vermont took home a big share of the $60,000 purse from a Colorado meet on February 19, 1982 after using "a new mind game," according to the following March issue of *Ski Racing*.

"All I did," Bruce is quoted as saying, "was program myself to win. The Silva Method teaches you through visual imagery to help yourself eliminate any negative thoughts . . . I just tell myself I am going to win, I imagine myself winning."

In the summer of 1975, the way the Chicago White Sox baseball players fared after taking the Silva Method was widely publicized on the CBS 60 Minutes television show, and on NBC's Today show. Each player's statistics before the Silva Method (the 1974 season) and after the Silva Method (the 1975 season) were compared. Each improved, most of them quite dramatically.

The increasing interest in sports and exercise of the past decade has been accompanied by an increased recognition of the important role the mind plays in physical matters. The sports literature is replete with references to mental attitudes and mental postures that enhance physical skill and physical endurance.

Early in this book, we asked you to throw a ball into a wastebasket first with failure pictures, then with success pictures. Mental pictures affect physical skills.

But that was just the beginning. From there, with practice in relaxing, practice in visualizing and imagining, practice in applying relaxed picturing to managerial skills, you are finding that mental pictures affect your control over your attitude, your energy, your concentration, your memory, your communications, your intelligence, your ability to instruct others, to solve problems, and to attain goals.

We doubt whether your success with the Silva Method will ever make the pages of *Time* Magazine or other media splashes. It is no longer news. Scores of stories were run in the 1970s. Today, millions of people are using the Silva Method. What else is new?

But this makes it all the more vital to every business executive that he know how to use more of his mind. To ignore this need is to be left behind.

ENHANCING GUT FEELINGS AND INTUITION

Philip L. had been using the Silva Method regularly for two years in managing his dry cleaning chain, when an opportunity arose demanding an immediate decision. A lease was available for a store in a building on a well-traveled highway. It was the right size, had fair rent, good parking. It had everything going for it—objectively. If he did not take it, another firm would. He had until noon that day to decide.

Philip went to his Alpha level sitting at his desk. He visualized the building and the particular store in it. He then moved the picture to the left. The building disappeared. He called up the agent. "I pass on this one," he told him. Within a year that building was destroyed by fire.

As you use the Alpha level to solve problems on a daily basis, over an extended period of time, you can take shortcuts in the methodology. For instance, programming at night to wake up at the appropriate time to work on a particular problem and then, on awakening, returning to your level, is still the recommended procedure, but it is no longer the only procedure.

Gradually you become more in control of your mind, and by merely beginning to visualize or imagine in a relaxed, daydreaming way, you automatically go to your level.

Sitting at your desk with a problem confronting you, you can imagine an expert on these matters sitting by your side. Ask him. Stop thinking. Resume thinking and the answer that comes is the solution to the problem.

Sitting at your desk with a choice of several alternatives, you can unfocus your eyes in a daydreaming way and use the elimination method, giving each a number, pairing them, and getting a mental answer as to which alternative is the best one for you to take.

There is never any substitute for Alpha, but the state of Alpha becomes easier to reach.

I can offer you no way to accelerate this. It comes with practice. I do know that it comes faster to those who go through the intensive Silva Method class training. Within a few weeks of daily use, many graduates can function at Alpha anywhere, anytime, and with their eyes open.

At that time, spontaneous gut feelings and perceptions become more frequent and dependable. It is as if the right hemisphere is taking a more active role in our thinking.

MAKING THE ROUTINE SUPERIOR

As the act of going to Alpha becomes habitual, it becomes more natural for you to use it. Whereas in the beginning, you use it because a serious problem exists or a profound decision must be made, after a while its use becomes less premeditated, so to speak. You just go to Alpha whenever the spirit moves you.

For instance, you can be doing some routine tasks where a certain amount of good judgment is needed. You have done these tasks satisfactorily before the Silva Method, many times. But now, with the Silva Method, you can do them even better. You can use the elimination method at Alpha in:

Pricing products
Setting manufacturing runs
Determining discounts to be allowed
Evaluating credit limits
Establishing budgets

The result will be a fine-tuning of your judgment. Routine matters, instead of being handled in a routine way, will enjoy the same superior touch as more important matters. But, routine matters occur more frequently. So the small increment of advantage you gain adds up rapidly. You begin to see it in the profit and loss statement.

Taking a deep breath, if preprogrammed, putting your three fingers together, also if preprogrammed, or unfocusing the eyes, can yield:

Better words and phrases in a letter or ad

The proper order of procedure in written material or activities

The diplomatic approach in conversation

The right area for a sales test

The best person to do a job

Major projects should always be handled at night in the manner previously described. Such projects usually need the most time to do this. They deserve the best you can give them.

This best is selected by your mind while you are asleep, awaking you at the appropriate time to reach the brain neurons involved and to permit your visualized and imagined scenes to zero in on their targets when those targets are most receptive.

HANDLING MAJOR CHANGES

There are no guarantees in the world of business. Jobs, products, and markets can change or disappear. Firms can fold. Industries can become obsolete. Wars and natural calamities can destroy. Governments can intervene.

Fortunately, we do not have these kinds of major problems to handle on a daily basis. But, just as fortunately, we have a tool to use when we need it—Alpha.

Major changes separate the men from the boys—and the women from the girls. The men and women are the clairvoyant ones. The boys and girls are not. The boys and girls are still using only a small fraction of their brains.

Managers need to be men and women in order to succeed in the changing times ahead. They need to be clairvoyant. They need to activate that clairvoyance on their own by using the proper procedures as presented in this book.

Clairvoyant managers must function in two dimensions. They must function in the subjective dimension—the world of the mind. They must function in the objective dimension—the world of the brain, body, and matter.

If you function in just the subjective dimension, you are nonproductive. If you function in just the objective dimension, you are noncreative. If you function in both dimensions, you are a productive problem solver.

For something to happen in the world of matter—your shop, your business, your plant, your practice—it must happen first in the world of the mind.

It happens in the world of the mind by first turning down the world of matter input—closing your eyes or unfocusing them. Then you visualize what you want to happen, feeling your desire, expectation, and belief.

Now you have triggered creative energy to go to work in the world of matter. Your project materializes.

The clairvoyant manager today must be able to work in this way. He does not have to *understand* these two worlds, philosophically or scientifically. He only needs to *use* them.

As Socrates said, "What is mind? It does not matter. What is matter? Never mind."

THE REALITY OF THE SUBJECTIVE DIMENSION

Everything that has been created in this material world was created first in the subjective world. This truism predates the Silva Method, predates civilization, predates all of history.

For business managers in the past to ignore the subjective dimension in their education and training has been a serious mistake for them and for business. But since practically everybody made that mistake, they got by.

Business managers are no longer making that mistake. The word is out. Subjective dimension training is here. Those who attempt "business as usual" in the years ahead will not get by.

The subjective dimension, once considered an unreal wasteland of the imagination, is now recognized as reality.

Being a pioneer in the activation of the subjective mind, I know about its reality more keenly than most people. I have used it in my life and in my business.

You hear of people getting laid off, companies closing down, entire cities being hit by economic hardship. Economic hardship is nothing new to me. In Laredo, Texas, times have always been hard for the majority of people. Yet there are always ways to cope.

You begin with a positive attitude—positive desire, positive expectation, positive belief. You follow that up with positive pictures, seeing your solution, seeing it getting under way, seeing it accomplished.

A man called me one night and said he had preprogrammed for a promotion and a raise. Instead, he complained bitterly, he got laid off. I have faith in programming. It is reality. He was interpreting the layoff as reality instead of expecting and believing that his mental pictures were the reality. I told him to keep programming.

A few days later he called to tell me that another company had hired him. It was a better job at higher pay. This company, he said, would not approach him while he worked for someone else. It was unethical. Getting laid off was the only way.

GENIUS IS REQUIRED

Average is no longer good enough. We are evolving. What is average today will be below average tomorrow. What is superior today will be average tomorrow. We are not on a merry-go-round where all you have to do is grab the brass ring. We are on a continuous forward motion. Mankind is evolving in consciousness. Stand still and you are left behind.

That evolution in consciousness is, at this moment in time, supplying us with right hemisphere control—the ability to tap powers of perception, intuition and creativity that are out of reach of the sensory-bound left brain.

In effect, this evolution in consciousness is giving us access to Higher Intelligence. We are realizing our role as co-creators.

We center our thinking by a sort of going within. We picture. We see what needs to be done. Then we do it.

Some of our creations are easier than others. The more difficult ones require perseverance. Perseverance provides reinforcement to the creative energy. The first time around, we plant the seeds. Perseverance fertilizes and waters, eventually bringing creations to fruition.

The clairvoyant manager is a genius. If today's manager is not clairvoyant and not a genius, he is going to be at a progressive disadvantage. The world of business is becoming more and more complicated. To be successful in this more complicated world, the business manager must be a genius.

What is a genius? A genius is a person who has learned to use the left brain hemisphere and the right brain hemisphere; a person who has enhanced the intuitive factor; a person who has developed visualization and imagination; a person who plants seeds in the subjective dimension and reaps harvests in the objective dimension; a person who thinks about the creation of a project first and then acts upon those thoughts.

THE SOURCE OF GENIUS

Economic pressures have sometimes forced people to look for supplemental sources of income. Then these supplemental sources surprisingly surpass the main source and become the full-time business.

It is as if an intelligence greater than our own was involved in the circumstances; perhaps the same intelligence that made my friend's programming for a raise result in the loss of his job so he could be offered a better job; perhaps the same intelligence that drove a Malaysian bank auditor to quit a lucrative position without a new one to step into, only to earn a $250,000 finder's fee a week later.

When I programmed for a dream to help me solve my money problem and dreamt of five numbers that turned out to be a winning lottery ticket, I had a distinct feeling that I was not the genius, that some other genius was at work.

Can we take credit for intuition? Or, does it come from a source outside of ourselves? We can take credit for our education, our learning, our experience, and for the ability to apply these to problems and circumstances. But can we take credit for unexplained perception, ESP, clairvoyance, psychic ability?

Enter Higher Intelligence.

One day we will understand better why putting the objective dimension on "hold" and activating the subjective mind gives us access to Higher Intelligence. In fact, it might take that Higher Intelligence for us to acquire that understanding.

Those who are satisfied to work at the objective level, as they are now, and take home that paycheck regularly may be enjoying a false sense of security. Life has a way of jolting the comfortable status quo.

"I don't need my subjective realm," they say. "Oh, yeah?" says life.

Access to Higher Intelligence is available for us for a reason. The reason can only be that we need it.

ACCELERATION OF CHANGE

The electronic age. The computerized office. The computerized industry. Interlocking systems. Manufacturing in space. Changes in the material dimension are coming faster and faster.

Today's business manager is no longer as secure within the four walls of his office as the day's routine would have him feel. Today's routine may be obsolete tomorrow—along with those individuals intent on retaining it.

Clairvoyance, once the handmaiden of mysticism, has come of age. Scientifically recognized in prestigious professional circles, and thoroughly mastered by the Silva Method training course, clairvoyance takes its place alongside education as a required tool for managers.

Education is the business manager's prime objective realm tool. Clairvoyance is the business manager's prime subjective realm tool. Experience is the business manager's prime tool for synthesizing the two realms.

With the subjective and objective realms working in concert through the business manager, no swift change can take him by surprise, no sudden shift can upset him, no wave of innovation can throw him.

It is now known that the left brain seems to specialize in

highly structured information. It can relate any stimulus instantly to what it already knows.

On the other hand, the right brain seems to specialize in material for which there has been no previous experience. It can instantly integrate new, diverse information.

In this changing world, Mr. or Ms. Manager, can you get by with only the left half of your brain?

WITH THE TRAINING COMPLETED

I am going to speak to you now as if you are a clairvoyant manager. I realize that some of you are reading this book before taking the concentrated Silva Method training course or before giving yourselves the training as set forth herein. Some of you may be partly along the way. Imagine that you have completed the training and that you are a clairvoyant manager.

When you imagine you are a working clairvoyant manager, here are some of the scenes that may come to mind:

- You arrive at the job feeling that you should have stayed in bed. You put your three fingers together, force a smile, and thump your thymus. In a minute or so, you are "a new person."

- Over the intercom, you are asked to please come to the executive vice president's office. You know it is about the cancellation of that big order. You take a deep breath, unfocus your eyes, and see the meeting taking place. In scenes, successively to the left, you see the meeting coming off constructively, and an amicable conclusion taking place. You go to the v.p.'s office. You put your three fingers together. You say the right thing. He is receptive. Together you work out a plan to recoup.

- Your foreman comes to your office. Yesterday you agreed to have lunch. You know what is on his mind. Last night you programmed to wake up at the right time. Back at your level, you programmed for handling the problem wisely. An expert in the personnel field assisted you at your level. You go to lunch. When you return, the disgruntled foreman is once again "gung ho!"

An Average Day

- "How's it going?" You have stopped to chat with a worker. He nods his head. You continue your walk. You have once again used a verbalized expression that you have programmed to help that worker to overcome a negative factor.

- You check out that man with a drinking problem. A bottle of cola is on his desk. You have programmed that each drink of cola is turning him more and more away from liquor. It is working well.

- You feel a headache coming on. You go to your Alpha level and review what needs to be done the rest of the day. In a few minutes, you end your session, without a headache.

- Your secretary cannot find a report. While she continues to look, you go to your level and visualize it. In the picture is another totally different report. You tell your secretary to get you that report. When she does, you find the missing report with it.

- At coffee break time, you decide to take an Alpha break instead. You go to your level, give yourself positive affirmations that include, "I am energetic, aware, and enthusiastic." You open your eyes feeling great.

- The weekly managers' meeting will take place in a few minutes. You have preprogrammed for your ideas to be well received. They are.

- From the meeting, there emerges the need to counteract your competitor's new strategy with a new strategy of your own. That night you program to awaken at the appropriate time. When you do, and go to your level, you invite the industry leader to advise you. Several ideas come to mind. You use the elimination method to select the best. You retain the others for future consideration. The next day, your proposal is accepted and implemented. You are commended.

Such scenes are now commonplace for you, a clairvoyant manager. It is your average day—no big thing.

TAKING ADVANTAGE OF CHANGE

Change is threatening. Most people are intimidated by something new. They feel safer and more comfortable with the status quo. Managers are no exception. For every business manager interested in this book and its teaching, there are ten who may dismiss it out of hand.

There is one change a person can make that will prepare him for all future changes. That change is: the change from being left brained to being right and left brained—to being mentally "ambidextrous."

The right brain accepts change. It thrives on change. Changes become changes for the better. That is because the right brain is the source of intuition, creativity, inspiration, and new ideas.

With the right brain going for you now, you are a versatile manager. You flow with change. Indeed, change becomes a challenge, to which you rise effectively. Others, who are less able to cope with change, lean on you. They depend on you for answers. You rise in their esteem. Even left brained directors vote for you, Mr. or Ms. Clairvoyant Executive, Mr. or Ms. Chairman of the Board.

TAKING ADVANTAGE OF CLAIRVOYANCE

In continuing my discussion with you, an accomplished clairvoyant, I hope you won't take offense at my talking to you now as a Dutch uncle.

It is a responsibility to be able to solve problems in genius-like ways and to create better products that do not hurt or kill, and find better ways of doing things.

Mankind has always had a choice to work for his own good or his own detriment. He has not always chosen his own good. Inherent in the Silva Method is a common goal: to strive to take part in constructive and creative activities in order to make this a better world to live in. We hope to leave behind a better world for those who follow.

Yes, we look out for number one—our self. But we also

look out for our family, helping them to cope with stress, to think positively, and to learn to activate more of their minds.

We also look out for our fellow workers, our company, our industry. We look out for our country and we program for human harmony and growth on planet Earth.

You can do all of those Alpha activities I listed a few pages ago and still have time to program at your level:

- For a perfect day for yourself

- For your children's success in school

- For your wife's health and happiness

- For your company president's wisdom

- For your state legislature to come to beneficial conclusions

- For Congress to act in the common welfare

- For the President and his Cabinet to work for the national good

- For the leaders of the world to be enlightened

- For the planet to revolve in love and harmony

Many Silva groups programmed for the safe return of the Iranian hostages. Many groups programmed for the successful conclusion of our various sorties into space. One group programmed for the end of an invasion of blackbirds that plagued an East Coast farm area for weeks; two hours later they were gone.

We are currently programming for a hospital where clairvoyants work side by side with physicians to help correct health problems. Watch for it.

We are also programming nationally for schools to use Silva Method techniques to enhance the learning process and make all students "superior human beings." Watch for this, too.

WHO ARE YOU?

My esteemed colleague, director, and lecturer Harry McKnight, has a way of asking his students "Who are you?" so that the answer is inherent in the question.

The students have already proved their clairvoyant ability. He points out what they were able to do. "When you are able to project your intelligence any distance, that is the quality of being infinite. When you can go forward or backward in time—eternal. When you can know something you have no way of knowing—omniscient. When you are able to correct problems or abnormalities—omnipotent." Then comes the question. "Infinite, eternal, omniscient, omnipotent—who are you?"

You can hear a pin drop.

Whoever you are, Higher Intelligence and you are related. All the great sages proclaimed in their own way that "The Father and I are one."

- In Buddhism: "Look within, thou art Buddha."

- In Hinduism, "Atman (individual consciousness) and Brahman (universal consciousness) are one."

- In Christianity, "The Kingdom of Heaven is within you."

- Mohammed said, "He who knows himself knows his lord." In the Upanishads, we read, "By understanding the Self all this universe is known."

- Saint Christopher said, "He who knows himself knows God."

I am honored to know you, Mr. Clairvoyant Manager. But more important, you should be honored to know yourself. You honor your body, you honor your family, you honor your company and, we hope, your country, and your world.

It is my personal wish that you also honor Higher Intelligence, that Higher Intelligence be grateful for your support.

The world is full of unfinished projects. We need to work on protecting the environment, on control of nuclear weapons, on hunger, on preservation of the species.

Excuse me, what did you say? You have a staff meeting in thirty minutes, and you wish to reinforce your programming for a successful outcome? Of course. I'll leave you. You have my warmest wishes.

"Five . . . Four . . . Three . . . Two . . . One . . ."

Index

221